"So often Christian books offer us a well-intended formula for healing—one we've heard so often, we've got it down pat. But what happens when the formula fails in real life? What happens when the right ingredients or the proper measures still leave us empty in despair instead of full with promise and hope? *Soul Bare* won't offer you a formula. You won't turn the final pages armed with a ready-made antidote for brokenness or a cure-all salve for sin. What you *will* find is raw realness: uncensored stories by real people wrestling with the grit of real life. Lean in deep to *Soul Bare*. Your wounds have a place here. Your heart will find a home between these pages. You will see your real self in these stories. And you will glimpse our real God."

Michelle DeRusha, author of *Spiritual Misfit*

"I held my breath, I cried, I shuddered, I whispered prayers, I ached. Most of all, I fell more deeply in love with Jesus through these words and stories. I can't help but think how wide and deep and long this love is that finds us all so broken and yet so beautiful."

Idelette McVicker, founder and editor-in-chief, *SheLoves Magazine*

"If you harbor any doubts that God is present in the broken places, let this prayerful chorus of voices dispel them. *Soul Bare* is a psalm to what is hard and holy, a glorious song of praise to a God who reaches into darkness and blesses even our deepest wounds."

Esther Emery, writer

"What does it mean to be 'authentic'? We give the word a lot of reverence, but actually stepping out in authenticity remains a frightening prospect for many of us. There are those parts of our lives that we would rather not acknowledge, that we would rather forget, that we assume would isolate us if they were found out. *Soul Bare* is proof that authenticity never isolates, but always invites new growth and community. Any reader is bound to find him- or herself in these pages somewhere."

Matt Appling, author of *Life After Art* and *Plus or Minus*

"Wading through the waters of *Soul Bare*, I felt I'd been entrusted with something precious. These pages are filled with the all-too-true and all-too-resonant stories of real people who have loved, lost, sinned, survived, hoped and healed. The fact that these contributors happen to be gifted writers only makes the reading that much better. They are in essence 'going first,' bringing their scars into broad daylight so the rest of us will follow—and Lord knows we need to. It's way too easy to hide behind small talk and Christian cliché. You can get away with it for quite a long time, but real life begins in real relationship. And relationships are born of vulnerability. We've got to learn to drop our masks and be human together. I'm grateful beyond words to the brave women and men who shared their humanity and God's goodness on the pages of this book. It's an absolute gift."

Christa Wells, award-winning singer-songwriter

"These stories are brave, honest and lyrical: a mosaic of shadows and light. As I turned these pages, I felt like I was being invited to glimpse a sacred cross section of the human experience. Suffering. Celebration. Despair. Hope. Sin. Forgiveness. And through it all an unmistakable thread of relentless redemption."

Micah J. Murray, writer

soul bare

Stories of Redemption by Emily P. Freeman,
Sarah Bessey, Trillia Newbell and more

edited by
CARA SEXTON

IVP Books

An imprint of InterVarsity Press
Downers Grove, Illinois

InterVarsity Press
P.O. Box 1400, Downers Grove, IL 60515-1426
ivpress.com
email@ivpress.com

InterVarsity Press® is the book-publishing division of InterVarsity Christian Fellowship/USA®, a movement
of students and faculty active on campus at hundreds of universities, colleges and schools of nursing in the
United States of America, and a member movement of the International Fellowship of Evangelical Students.
For information about local and regional activities, visit intervarsity.org.

All Scripture quotations, unless otherwise indicated, are taken from THE HOLY BIBLE, NEW
INTERNATIONAL VERSION®, NIV® Copyright © 1973, 1978, 1984, 2011 by Biblica, Inc.™
Used by permission. All rights reserved worldwide.

While any stories in this book are true, some names and identifying information may have been changed to
protect the privacy of individuals.

Published in association with MacGregor Literary, Inc.

Cover design: Cindy Kiple
Interior design: Beth McGill
Images: © Rosie Ann Prosser / Trevillion Images

ISBN 978-0-8308-4326-8 (print)
ISBN 978-0-8308-9439-0 (digital)

Printed in the United States of America ∞

 As a member of the Green Press Initiative, InterVarsity Press is committed to protecting
the environment and to the responsible use of natural resources. To learn more, visit
greenpressinitiative.org.

Library of Congress Cataloging-in-Publication Data
Names: Freeman, Emily P., 1977- author. | Sexton, Cara, editor.
Title: Soul bare : stories of redemption / by Emily P. Freeman, Sarah Bessey,
    Trillia Newbell and more ; edited by Cara Sexton.
Description: Downers Grove : InterVarsity Press, 2016. | Includes
    bibliographical references.
Identifiers: LCCN 2016010697 (print) | LCCN 2016011635 (ebook) | ISBN
    9780830843268 (pbk. : alk. paper) | ISBN 9780830894390 (eBook)
Subjects: LCSH: Christian life—Meditations.
Classification: LCC BV4501.3 .F73934 2016 (print) | LCC BV4501.3 (ebook) |
    DDC 248.8/6—dc23
LC record available at http://lccn.loc.gov/2016010697

P   21   20   19   18   17   16   15   14   13   12   11   10   9   8   7   6   5   4   3   2   1
Y   34   33   32   31   30   29   28   27   26   25   24   23   22   21   20   19   18   17   16

For you, dear reader,

and all the soul-bare stories

that whisper the truth

of a wild and beautiful you

CONTENTS

Part Three: Hope and Healing

INTRODUCTION

Dear Reader-Friend,

There's a lot of talk about authenticity out there. A lot of feverish cheerleading about being real, showing our messy selves and holding one another up while doing it. But I've withdrawn into listening for a while, sort of taking things in while I withdrew somewhat from the cacophonous conversations about authenticity, even as I fought my own obstacles to bring a book about it into the light of day. It's been a time when my own shadows hovered darker, my darkest clouds loomed closer than ever, and I had to squint to see Truth within and between all the well-meaning voices of Christendom, even in all its beauty. What I have seen is that there is a lie so many of us believe: *Your wounds have no place here.*

Yet there are times when the Christian community is all that stands between me and hopelessness—days when friends and soul companions reach across the distance and transform it into a tabernacle where we gather and laugh, or mourn, or shake our fists together. I know what beauty looks like when I see it. This is beauty. It always has been. It always will be.

There are different kinds of truth telling. There's a height above laundry piles and laughter. There's a depth below bad-hair days and fast-food confessions. When I said yes to coordinating a book about authenticity, about the raw and real baring of our souls for a holy, redemptive purpose, I did so without anything in particular to say but with an open heart to see what he had to show me. I did so because this project was his from the beginning. It has always been his. And now, three years after God stirred my own scarred and broken heart with the whisper of his love for the scarred and broken depths of yours, I know one thing I didn't know when I started. It is something I think you'll come to know, too, as you recognize familiar faces and familiar shadows that challenge even the most radiant countenance among us.

> No, in all these things we are more than conquerors through
> him who loved us. For I am sure that neither death nor life,
> nor angels nor rulers, nor things present nor things to come,
> nor powers, nor height nor depth, nor anything else in all
> creation, will be able to separate us from the love of God in
> Christ Jesus our Lord. (Rom 8:37-39 ESV)

You've heard the verses before. You may have even sung the songs. But do you *know* this, really, to be true? Do you know that your wounds, too, are welcome? Do you know that the soul-bare places, the sights and sounds of your life that you shelter from public display, belong to him? That he resides there? That he *redeems* there? My prayer for you, reader, is that you do. That you always will. And that these pages will remind you.

The stories that follow were each written by a different author, all of them telling their own redemptive soul-bare truth. These have been broken up into three sections to help you navigate through the book: Part One: Letting Go, Part Two: Leaning In, and Part Three: Hope and Healing. At the end of the book is a bio section that tells a little about the authors and where else you can find their work. Each of these writers is blessing the world with their words, and I encourage you to visit their blogs, buy their books, and otherwise support the important work they are doing by honoring their writing gifts, and then to keep the conversation open by telling your own soul-bare stories.

To tell our truth is to link arms across the divides that keep us out, to close the gaping lie that says our wounds do not matter. Together we are a living mosaic—a tiled path winding through the beauty and pain of human experience and leading toward redemption, and this book, together with your own soul-bare story, is a work of art that speaks of forgiveness, grace and healing. We tell the stories of life and love, bound together in the perfection and completion of Christ's great sacrifice. The very Word of God is, after all, a collection of broken stories about broken people just like us. Your story is your own and has been written by the Creator with purpose. Even if your edges are chipped, your story is beautiful. Tell it.

In his love and light, standing soul bare beside you,
Cara

Part One

L LETTING GO

MORE FOR YOU THAN THIS

Shannan Martin

2008

Spring descends in its usual way, slow and seductive, singing me awake from months of face-smacking cold and lake-effect snow, promising that while all good things come to an end, so do the bad.

Our six acres of pasture are as green to me as motherhood, each splintered fence post, every sweep of a sudsy cloth over chubby arms waking me up to who I was made to be. After years of waiting, I am a mommy to Calvin and Ruby. After years of working and saving, I'm a wanna-be woman of the uncertain frontier, rising up to work the land we'd fought so long to own.

Truth rings a bell—I am ill-equipped to manage both perennial beds and potty-training. But this is the life I always wanted, so I reach out and touch its reverb, quieting my doubts, absorbing their song until naptime, when I tuck my one-year-old and three-year-old into their beds and make a beeline for some quiet. *Hush, little ones, we're safe here. You can rest now. We're home.*

Pulling rain boots onto my feet, I catch my breath along the west row of pines, where redemption takes shape in the melting snow and the only thing demanding my attention is the slim neck of a hyacinth, the lifted lips of a newborn crocus. Every step is discovery, uncovering more of the treasure I've been given: the love, the children, the drafty farmhouse, the crumbling barns, the land, *the life*.

I'm uncovering gratitude in the slope of a roofline, finding my roots among the oaks. My eyes know only hope. My heart keeps company with the security of our simple life.

2010

Two years later to the month, almost everything is changing. We both heard the whisper. We both turned around, walked away, refused to believe the words were true, or for us. *I have more for you than this.*

More? Impossible.

The whisper chips away our control with its persistence, doubling efforts to jarring effect as we fly across the world then back home, a broken-hearted toddler with pain in his almond eyes raging in our arms.

It's just the beginning but, thank God, we have no clue. Had the shock waves not been meted out, they surely would have broken us.

Day bleeds into night and back again, the edges of every sure thing warping around us until our world no longer stands erect. Morning comes each day with a vengeance, and we stir sorrow into the tea that scalds our throats the whole way down.

Our precious baby stares back at us—strangers—and we try not to long for easier days. The hours are clocked as over and over he brings us his tiny, Korean soccer shoes or his corduroy coat. These are his closest companions, the remnants of what he lost in order for our prayers to be answered. His eyes wear mourning shrouds, pulsing grief beyond their years. *Let me go home.*

We are home, but Silas is not, and the ground tremors beneath the weight of this truth.

Life is no longer simple. Security is irrelevant, so far away that we wonder if we'd ever known it all, or if we would recognize it if it returned.

One month passes, and our reward is the sudden loss of my job.

Four more weeks, and our words to our two oldest children are spent in promises we do not dare allow ourselves to believe. *Things will soon be normal again.* We want to rock Silas in the turquoise chair, to sing into his ear, to sniff the top of his head. We want him to hold our hand, but he shakes it loose. At less than two years old, he feels safer in the corner of his room than in our arms.

We are given another gift, one we don't recognize as grace: my husband's sturdy career in federal politics is over, abruptly and with finality, a decade of expert rung-climbing knocked to its knees in the wake of another man's scandal. An unseen force begins siphoning our meticulously drawn and executed financial safety net through a hidden drain at the bottom of our life. The things we held closest to our chest, the ones that made us feel smart and responsible, become slippery in our hands.

Ever slowly, painfully human, we begin to see from all sides the truth we were handed: God *does* have more for us, and often, his more looks like less.

It can look like loss and pain.

From the vantage point of God's kingdom set on the face of this wobbly earth, the very best he has to offer can look like surrender and taste like tears. It sounds like a for-sale sign being driven into dirt and feels like walking in reverse.

Our farmhouse is on the market, the one we swore we would never leave. God wants more. He wants everything we were taught to want: our ego, our DIY security, our account balances, our dreams. Silas is teaching us in baby steps how to cozy up to pain. Now we see it everywhere. Our job is to love our neighbor, to care for the poor, to align with the low. We've chosen the world and called it our religion. We have served an unholy trinity of cash, security and staus quo.

Oh, to have our conscience quelled, to unsee and unknow what had never for a moment left the pages of the book we said we loved.

What good is a faith that inverts the paradigm, putting God at the center of *my* will? Why did the Sunday school Jesus never talk about losing my life for his sake? Decades of church membership and dutiful rule following had done nothing to prepare us for wherever God is leading.

I try to fend off the fear snaking our way. I fight my own heart. I'm Lot's wife, already turning around, and I'm not even gone.

A soundtrack assembles of naysayers, doubters and punks. Most of them mean well, but our hearts split and scab, then split again. They say we've lost our minds, and my pride quietly leans their way. But just past the double-paned kitchen window of the home we've been asked to leave, my baby loses himself for a moment in a game of chase with his new brother and sister. His courage yanks a thread deep inside me, and my fingers unfurl. Maybe I don't want to be the one deciding my future. Maybe that's all I need to know for now.

Locking eyes with my youngest son through the glass, it's clear—we all need help remembering how to trust.

2012

We clear the table in a hurry, dinner plates rinsed, leftovers snapped under lids, the clatter of three young kids ricocheting off close quarters. Summer's long days are losing their steam, the leaves of the maples hinting at gold. And the air? Well, it's perfect. The buzz from the park positioned just across the street floats through the screens, a unique torture when you're eight or six or four.

It's only been two months, but this is already home. Our old, farmhouse art hangs on the walls as proof, and a new path is being worn between our house and the one next door. Ruby picks up Spanish phrases in her kindergarten class at the school just two blocks down. Neighbors knock on our door well past bedtime.

These are the weeks of discovering which parts of us work and what needs to go. We're all a bit at sea, but we're here together, and we're still *us*.

I'm still prone to waxing poetic about the sleepy turning of a rose. I like to talk peanut butter cake as much as I used to. But I couldn't have guessed how I was made for life on the wrong side of the tracks. Give me street art, cussing teenagers, neighbors with laundry carts and nicotined fingertips. Show me what's real. I can take it. I *prefer* it. My blissful farm-girl life pointed me toward simple gratitude so that now, right here, I recognize its reflection on the blister and burn of days spent banging against the pain of another.

Looking hard in the mirror, I hunt down my humanity and put it on trial. I confront my ugliness, the drip and drear of a misspent life. I think long on what really matters when it comes to this one life on earth.

The chaff is being shucked. We don't want it. We shove away our old pretenses, our ego, our better judgment, and trade them for risk, the threat of judgment and the certainty that we'll never explain it well enough. Laying down my peace-keeping armor, I find who I was always meant to be, a woman who knows no bravery apart from God, a girl desperate to be saved. Let the opinions and disappointments fall around my ankles like spent petals. For the first time, I don't care.

We are simply here to be neighbors, to choose a place not accustomed to being chosen. We're still introverted and awkward, with normal jobs and kids who gripe. We don't have time to anticipate all the mistakes we'll make, and we sure won't offer predictions about the future. This woman with her color-coded plans and ten-year goals is tired of getting it wrong, and besides, the park is booming and we're racing daylight.

A train screams down the tracks like one thousand breaking hearts, but across the street, kids squeal, their legs pumping them higher into the sky. Little girls dangle from monkey bars, rowdy boys take up fallen walnuts as free-range ammo.

So long, quiet, long-lane evenings.

Calvin and Ruby race to meet friends you'd think they've known forever. Silas hangs back, full of four-year-old questions and the occasional protest.

The three of us lag behind: Daddy, Silas and Mommy, a silhouette of grace against the low-setting sun.

Somewhere in the thrum of neighborhood living, I catch a familiar tune. *I still have more for you.*

The truth sets a fire in my bones. More often it looks different than we imagined, but I'm not afraid anymore.

"Swing me into the air!" Silas shouts. And we do.

He never lets go of our hands.

DARK CLOUDS AND ABUNDANT GRACE

Trillia J. Newbell

DARK, THUNDEROUS CLOUDS fill the sky. Even the slightest glimpse of sunshine is quenched by the cumulonimbus.

You take a step of faith and walk outside. Big balls of frozen ice begin to fall, hitting you one by one. It hurts. It doesn't make sense.

Keep walking...

The dark clouds seem to close in around you. Each step is harder and more treacherous.

Keep walking...

The further you walk, the harder it gets. "This plodding is so rot with pain," you mumble as you look ahead.

There in the distance is a ray of sunlight. You remember that beautiful inheritance. You know it's coming.

Keep walking...

It's an act of valiant faith to put one foot in front of the other,

Keep walking...

You're going to make it to the end. Weak. Tired. But hopeful, because of that little ray, that faint but sure ray.

Keep walking.

And when you get there you'll realize, he has always been there.

That scene above is a familiar theme of my short life. Trial after trial, the Lord reminds me of his faithfulness, of his steadfast love. Joy comes in the morning, but the morning doesn't always come within eight hours of the sun setting. Dark clouds have filled my days, and I've often wondered if they'd overwhelm me.

The clouds crowded me when my best friend, my father, passed from this earth and into another. I would never see his bright eyes and handsome grin again. I wouldn't get the joy of racing him across the parking lot. The drumbeats that would fill the living room from nothing more than his thighs and knees is now a faint memory. How he could make such sounds from his quads I'll never really know.

The clouds crowded me when an older man that a group of my friends trusted invaded my space and my innocence. It was a strange way to wake up—a stranger's hands in places meant only for my future husband. But the most excruciating pain was watching his wife on the stand in the courtroom explain that he was doing better—he had stopped molesting his two children. The clouds were dark over my head that day.

The clouds crowded me six sweet weeks after my husband and I welcomed the news of our first child with joy that we were sure the heavens could feel. We walked in the doctor's office eager to hear the subtle sound of a heart that had been ignited by our God. We had heard that the beats of those tiny hearts were fast—like little flutters. But we didn't hear a heartbeat, and we had to experience the agony of that loss three additional times.

Oh, dark clouds have most definitely covered my head. But like the psalmist in Psalm 121 I cry out:

> I lift up my eyes to the hills.
>> From where does my help come?
> My help comes from the LORD,
>> who made heaven and earth.
> He will not let your foot be moved;
>> he who keeps you will not slumber.
> Behold, he who keeps Israel
>> will neither slumber nor sleep.
> The LORD is your keeper;
>> the LORD is your shade on your right hand.
> The sun shall not strike you by day,
>> nor the moon by night.
> The LORD will keep you from all evil;
>> he will keep your life.
> The LORD will keep
>> your going out and your coming in
>> from this time forth and forevermore. (ESV)

God knew about my dark clouds. He knew that I would mourn and weep. God reminds me in his Word that he is my Father. Where does my help come from? It comes from my Father. Each cloudy day brought a ray of hope. Joy comes in the morning. Does God change our circumstances? Sometimes. But more than not, he changes our perspective. He changes our hearts. When I felt empty, he filled me with more of himself.

God doesn't promise to take away difficult circumstances, but he does promise to be your keeper. Joy is not an artificial happiness. Joy comes from a deep trust in our holy, good, sovereign God. Joy is rest. Resting in him, our Father, our keeper. He is our sustainer of life. We can jump and play because we know that the mighty and holy one is on our side. He draws near to us. He tells you to come, oh weary soul, and he will give you rest (Mt 11:28). The rest will bring peace and joy—joy that we'll experience forevermore.

Forevermore. That is our hope. Not that our joy will come here and now but that he will one day wipe away every tear and mourning will be no more. Hope is that one day we'll see our Savior face to face. He is making all things new. And on that day, we will experience a joy that will be indescribable. Those dark clouds will be no more. He longs for us to lift up our eyes and remember where our help comes from. Remember our inheritance and the promises he's provided for us in his Word. Those are for you and me—today. Right now. Yes, even you right now can experience joy—sorrowful, yet always rejoicing.

Hymn writer William Cowper once wrote that the dark clouds would break with blessings on your head. He was right. The clouds that we so dread have a purpose. The blessing could simply, yet profoundly, be experiencing more of Jesus. We may not receive all the answers this side of eternity, but may it be that we can say, blessed be the name of the Lord!

If you find yourself in the deepest of darkest clouds searching for joy, ask the Lord who gives abundantly to those who ask. He has grace stored up for you, for this occasion. His grace will sustain you and will bring you out of the despair. His grace is what allows us to say, yes, I am joyful. Not because of anything in me or in my strength but because I have a God who is keeping me, strengthening me and reminding me of my great hope. Joy does come in the morning.

COLD, DARK GROUND

Jennifer J. Camp

*For the mind set on the flesh is death, but the
mind set on the Spirit is life and peace.*

ROMANS 8:6 NASB

FIFTEEN YEARS OLD and my back aches from gray rock pressing underneath the thin blanket from the trunk of his car. The creek bed sits dry, and I am above it, lying pressed flat next to a partially paved dirt road. The road my family drove on to picnic in these same, sloped hills at Easter. The road my grandfather swerved off of wildly, with grandkids next to him, for fun, in his white Dodge pickup with the bouncy seats. It is just me now, denim skirt too short, tank top stretched against barely tan skin, and the boyfriend I convinced myself last year I would marry. How else to explain a good girl, the granddaughter of the town doctor with the good grades and Sunday school reputation, making out with the too-tall basketball player in the silver Camaro?

I shouldn't be here. Not like this.

I don't remember any inner struggle about whether or not to go through with this. It seemed inevitable, this choice hardly a choice at all. My dad's voice at the dinner table years ago, the only "sex ed" talk I can ever remember having with my family, running like a tape through my head: "Good girls don't kiss boys until they get married."

But I was never the girl they thought I was, and nothing makes it clearer than the confusion of this fifteen-year-old girl hiding in the foothills on rock-strewn dirt, watching wild California oaks frame a starless black sky.

As a teenager I didn't believe I had what it took to be popular and have a group of close friends. I believed I wasn't interesting enough, smart enough, witty enough or funny enough. From the lie that I didn't have a voice—manifesting from years of being told I was quiet by well-meaning adults outside my family—to my refusal to believe I was capable of writing my own eighth-grade valedictorian graduation speech haunted me. I didn't believe I had words, so I borrowed another's. I didn't believe I was good enough to be liked and accepted just as I was. How could I possibly be loved?

Being physically intimate with boys became a way for me to find and gain attention I felt I didn't deserve. Having a boyfriend meant I was desired and worthy of being pursued. Offering physical intimacy, I believed, would make a boy stick around. I was shy in group gatherings, but offering myself sexually to a boy made me feel empowered. Sex became a way that I could control people—these boys and these relationships. I liked that sex made me feel worthy and strong.

Months after losing my virginity in the dry California foothills, I became pregnant. I read the thin blue line on the white plastic stick in disbelief and horror a few days before school let out for Christmas vacation. The next night, panicked and terrified, I ran down my driveway in my thin blue and gold polyester basketball uniform, still on from a late night game. I sought solace in the orchard that was my childhood playground, the wonderland of beauty my dad planted and that framed our country home.

Immune to the cold and the frost on the ground, I flung myself under one of the leafless branches blending in the black December sky. I screamed for freedom, hope, another chance— longing for life.

Low self-worth and the idol of self can breed inauthenticity, silence and shame. When pride becomes an idol, the soul cannot bear the weight of truth until the old self is laid on the block and killed.

In C. S. Lewis's *The Great Divorce*, we see beauty of redemption when angels invite visitors to heaven who would otherwise stay in hell, apart from God. They are invited one by one to let Jesus set them free of their false selves and live, finally, in heaven with Jesus. Angels reveal the horror of the people's sins, and the desolation that remains when they continue to pick up lies and reject truth.

In one situation, a man's struggle with lust is manifested as a lizard clinging to his shoulder, whispering lies into his ear. The lizard's voice is familiar, and the man seems incapable of separating lies from truth. The whispers of deception feel a part of him and he can't imagine letting the angel rid him of the lizard, creepy as it is. The man panics at the angel's insistent request: "May I kill it?" But the man is afraid, believing the lizard's lies that he will die too if the lizard is taken away.

There is such horrific danger in clinging to our false selves. Unless we surrender and abandon these lies, these idols, these false selves to Jesus, we are the man with the decaying lizard on his shoulder, thinking the way without Jesus is best, that it is better for sin to remain. Silence about our sin births only further darkness. We lie writhing and desolate on cold, hard ground.

While my parents thought I was Christmas shopping with my boyfriend, I visited a clinic and had an abortion. I was grateful I did not need my parents' approval so no one would ever have to know. Shame, fear, pride and rebellion all outweighed preservation of life. Silence does not preserve life; it only kills.

Two decades after keeping my abortion a secret, God stirred me awake, beginning a journey in me both beautiful and painful, healing and hard. One evening, four new friends came over to pray for me, and Jesus invited me back to the dirt in the orchard. He showed me himself under the almond tree, the moment I turned away from him and decided to have an abortion. He sat with me under the almond tree while I shunned him, eyes full of tears, never turning, shining light in a dark night.

What does it mean to preserve a life? To hang on tightly to what we think is ours? To fight for what we believe in? To have all actions we take and words we say be for the purpose of self-preservation?

I imagine the answer depends on what it is we are trying to preserve—and whether or not it is worth it. And, maybe most importantly, whether what we are trying to preserve is true or false.

In C. S. Lewis's story, the man relents and the angel reaches out his flaming hands to fight for freedom from the lies that whisper and attempt to drown out the truth of God. From a red oily reptile now broken-backed on the ground, the lizard transforms into a silver-white stallion that carries the now beautifully transformed man on his back. With the angel standing by, they ride deeper into heaven. Only when lies are abandoned and truth adopted can the man discover his true strength and know the heart of God.

Believing a lie and living it out as truth causes ripples of heartache and destruction that can never be undone. The crux is that the lie, the thing that brings about the pain, is what Jesus died for—and we must surrender the lie to him to experience the beginning of life.

Inauthenticity, hiding and pretending to be someone we are not, leads to shame. Refusing to be vulnerable for the sake of preserving pride and self-image destroys the possibility of living in Jesus' freedom and joy and hope.

Lies breed lies—nothing good, nothing salvageable, nothing that breathes. But I know where truth begins now: Jesus with me, underneath an almond tree, his arms around a desperate daughter, reaching to soften, to bring warmth and to redeem cold, dark ground.

TOWERS AND CANYONS

Serena Woods

I HAD AN AFFAIR. It's one of three pivotal moments of my life. The other two are when I was adopted at age ten and when I became a mother at age nineteen. My affair is up there because it cracked open my life in such a way that when I healed, I was put back together better than I was before.

I've always had an idea of the type of woman who would do something that disgraceful, but I wasn't that type of woman. I actually loved Jesus, had some class and wanted nothing more than to be pure. Sin bears the fruit of faulty belief, and my affair revealed that I had some deeply ingrained false belief about God and myself. My childhood left me feeling filthy. I was adopted into an extremely religious and legalistic family. Religion made me feel so guilty that I gave up on my future and myself when I left home at seventeen. When I became a mother, I turned to God to help me rebuild what was left of my life, but I didn't know that I didn't have to earn my way into his heart until I did something that seemed unforgivable.

Seeds of false beliefs are planted when we're young. A child's mind is fertile soil; it soaks up whatever it walks through. Experiences are filtered through naive logic, and black and white reason gives cause to effect. We care for things that have value, so according to a child's reasoning, if you are not cared for then you must not have value. Reason and logic are the seeds in the soil that become the fruit-bearing crops of the adults they become. We can't always tell whether weeds or wheat are growing until it blooms. We can't tell if children blame themselves for their pain until we see what their lives later produce.

During my childhood, survival was the moment-to-moment goal, so love was in recession. My mother and I lived on the streets and survived any way we could. I stayed hidden while she worked. I scrounged through broken glass looking for my reflection while my mother entertained strangers for money. I was looking for proof that I existed, and my mother was looking for proof that she did too.

As I grew into an adult, the seeds of damage took root and grew with me. Weeds would emerge at times, and I would lose sight of my potential. My adult life became a twisted bramble of a child's logic and a devil's lie. I believed that I wasn't lovable. Spending much of my childhood in foster homes, I believed I was an unwanted burden. As someone with no roots and no family, I always felt invisible.

I didn't realize that believing love was rare made it something I couldn't pass up. I didn't know that trying to never need anyone kept me from healthy relationships, or that feeling invisible was coupled with a lack of responsibility for my own actions.

My affair ended two marriages and forged three new ones that produced two children. Enough distance between then and now has given me insight and peace, but those two were absent when I was in the middle of the horror of what I had done. I was careless and detached from reality when I was sneaking around, but I was fully aware of the hell I opened within me when reality caught up.

It doesn't matter that we all have damage. It's still hard to breathe when we see our own damage burn down the village. I know I'm not the only one with matches. I'm not the only garden plagued with weeds, but when your time comes, you're not thinking about anyone but yourself. It's personal.

I've lived through so many traumas that I have a library of Things I've Survived. This trauma is documented and put on leisure with the rest of them. I sit in a life I don't deserve, and it's when I have to write about what happened that I pull out my old memories and put on my old lenses. Looking at life from that perspective still pains me. I had such little faith in the salvation power of Jesus that I had a very real encounter with the torment of hell for a bit.

I've aged a little, but remembering my sin will always bring a somber quiet to me. The sorrow is a vastness I don't often visit, but my towers of joy are dependent on my canyons of sorrow. The paradigm of repentance is that one would not exist without the other.

I got over what people thought of me pretty quickly. The real pain came when my faith in Jesus was put to the test. It wasn't that I didn't believe in him in general; it was that I didn't believe in him *for me*. The fight for my spiritual loyalty was toxic to my psyche. I had to choose myself or him. It seems simple enough, but I should explain that I would have made myself pay for what I did. I hated myself.

I was the adulterous woman for whom Jesus was standing. He didn't have to convince other people to forgive me. He had to convince *me*. There is no sufficient way for me to tell you how that kind of love quaked me until I split open. Every avenue I once used to get to God was no longer open to me. I was kicked out, dismissed and excommunicated. Every Christian song on the radio, book on the shelf and sermon I could remember never spoke to the sinner. It spoke to the victim. Marketed Christianity, I learned, was about saving Christians. But here was Jesus, standing with his feet next to mine. Immanuel was justifying *me*.

I have had to watch as people face their own test of faith to even grasp what he did for me. Every good thing crumbled, and the cinderblock church halls echoed the most haunting silence. I used to think people were rejecting me when they were actually rejecting what he did for me. So much love in the face of so much distaste. In all my early Christian years, not once did I hear anything that would save me when I needed it. I don't blame them for not knowing that the ideal they uphold is real.

Night would scratch down my walls and I would hear him whisper, "This is why I came." Hell would roll through me like a swollen sea and he would whisper, "I haven't lost you." Towers of joy and canyons of sorrow were forged in me on those nights when the accuser spoke the truth and the Savior justified it all.

If I hadn't fallen, I would still be running. I would still be hiding my damage and trying to pretend I was whole. Only God can take evil intent and turn it into the very thing that saved me. All of me. If he can do it for me, then he can do it for anybody.

My experience with grace and the explicit message it sends is a constant tug on my soul to be a different kind of voice that may, one day, be found by another fallen like me. I know there are others who carry the weight of their sin as though there were some way they could earn their way back.

My message to them is simple. It's what Jesus said to me. He hasn't lost you and he'll never let you go. Your sin is not yours to carry. Your weeds bloomed and knocked over your world, but any world built on lies was never meant to stand. The only truth is him. Everything, even the perfection you've created and almost maintained, has to bow to him. Your failure is not an accident. God planned for it, and the plan's name is Jesus.

CAPTIVITY

Kris Camealy

I WANTED TO GO TO SCHOOL to design clothes. That was the plan—well, that was *my* plan before God interrupted. Applications rolled in, piling up on my desk, a burgeoning tower of opportunity and dreams yet to be realized, yet somewhere in the midst of all of this, the plan changed. One afternoon, as I sat on my floor amid the stacks of brightly colored sales pitches for various colleges and universities, I knew suddenly that I would not pursue design school in New York as I had originally imagined. Instead, I was drawn to a small Christian school situated practically on the white shores of the Gulf Coast. I heard the call to this place in my spirit. I cannot explain it, other than to describe it as an unexpected sense of peace—a knowing, soul-deep. That afternoon, I threw all of the other applications away and filled out just this one.

My parents, faithful at allowing me to make my own mistakes, questioned the changing plan without discouraging me from pursuing it. At seventeen, I was new to the faith, just two years a Christian, zealous and eager for more of the things of

God. I see now how simplistic my understanding of God was in those days, how very small he seemed to me then. But at the time, my excitement over my fledgling faith drowned out my naiveté. This sudden shift in direction made sense; I loved God, and so I should find a place to learn where I would be surrounded by others who love God as well. I suppose I failed to imagine that God could also be at a design school in New York. In those days, I imagined that God's presence was best experienced in the company of other believers. I went where I felt I could most easily find God. Within hours of arriving on the campus of my new home, I realized I had made a terrible miscalculation. This supposed utopia on the shores of the turquoise waters of the Gulf lacked the joy and grace I had tasted back home. Instead, a heavy emphasis was placed on obeying rules and living within the letter of the law.

My certainty about having been *called* to this school wavered almost as soon as we passed through the gates and headed toward registration. My all-girls dorm would become a prison the moment my parents left me there, after we'd already broken the sacred "no members of the opposite sex" rule and had my *father* into my room to help carry boxes. Looking at a trunk loaded down with boxes and suitcases, my dad immediately bucked at this rule and strode in, arms full of boxes and dresses, the weight of my new life. While men were not allowed in the dorms (let alone into our rooms), we ignored the signs and bore the burns of the awkward stares in the elevator. I immediately noticed the way the girls huddled in the corner when he rode up with me. I imagined they'd likely whisper about this new rebel on the fourth floor—they had me in their sights within my first fifteen minutes of entering this desert territory.

I learned a new rhythm there. Mornings started at 6 a.m. as my three roommates and I would rotate through the shower and wipe down the bathroom for "white glove" check. We took turns, each of us assigned to clean the mirrors, countertops, trash cans and so on. Room check included making your bed and leaving no clutter dispersed about the room. Anything out of place or not up to standard would result in demerits that would have to be reconciled at the end of the week when we'd file like prisoners through the demerit hall. There we were offered an opportunity to confess and explain our insubordination and receive our due punishment.

The days spun me dizzy in a slow-slipping spiral, with all of the theology I'd known being questioned and smothered just weeks into the semester. While demerits stacked up, I began to fail my classes. Surely this voluntary imprisonment had been a grievous mistake. I wondered if I had misread the feeling I had sensed so strongly all those months ago when I laid aside my dream of going to design school. Though I lived within minutes of some of the most beautiful beaches in the country, school rules made it virtually impossible to go. In order to leave campus a myriad of permission forms needed to be approved, and even with proper documentation, requests could still be denied by the administration. If I had managed a trip to the beach, my clothing limitations presented severe challenges to finding suitable beach attire. Female students were required to wear pantyhose at all times and knee length dresses or skirts. Even if I had tried to go to the beach, the potential fun would have melted away while I sat sweltering in knee-length shorts.

With virtually every minute of my day scheduled out for me, I lacked the freedom I imagined my peers were enjoying at their liberal arts schools of choice. I had enjoyed a myriad of plentiful freedoms at home under my parents' roof, which now ceased to exist for me.

A growing rebellion swelled within my spirit. My flesh followed suit. Scanning the rulebook, I searched for ways to push back within the limits and to break the spirit of the rules openly, defiantly, yet still be within the measure of the law. With rules regarding everything from acceptable hairstyles to appropriate shoes (no open toes, and sandals only with hosiery), I twisted the intent of their mandates into knots and wore them proudly in the form of electric blue tights and *just* long enough skirts. I teetered on the edge of what was permissible, pushing back against the tight restraints of the misshapen, misinterpreted and mishandled Levitical mandates. As it turned out, their rule about tights didn't specify *acceptable* patterns, and when I walked arrogantly through that main hall, my electric blue and neon green fishnets landed me smack in front of the administrator's reprimanding glare at the disciplinary board. I'd been "campused," which meant I couldn't get out from behind the gates for a set amount of time. My demerits administrator reminded me that I was just a few demerits shy of being "shunned" by my peers—a designation which wouldn't have mattered since I already felt completely alone.

In the hours between dinner and "lights out" I slipped into the stairwells. The concrete prayer room had a door and a tiny window that looked out on the hallway. The space resembled a prison cell with its bare concrete walls and dim lighting, but it was the only place I felt free on that campus. Opening my old youth group binder, I'd thumb the pages for the lyrics of my favorite worship songs and I'd sing—a canary deep in the bowels of this graceless cave. When I didn't know the words, I hummed the tune, trusting that God heard what I could not say. I read my Bible and wrote for hours there until they'd call me out for bed. With my every move monitored, and nearly every minute of my day regulated under the watching eyes of campus spies, the stairwell prayer room became my sanctuary, a private place where I could worship God with the lyrics and songs that had first wooed me to him. This was the only time I felt his presence in this place.

ESCAPE

As it happened when I'd chosen and accepted a place at that private college my father also received military orders to move to a base within forty-five minutes of that very school. At the time of this news I'd been sickened. I wanted to go *away* to school, and now my parents would be just a short drive away. But what felt like a damper on my much-anticipated college experience turned out to be one of the greatest gifts God could have given me during those four months at that school. With my parents close by, I had been able to leave the "prison" nearly every weekend. God knew I'd need them, and the provision of his perfect plan remained a hopeful sliver of his grace and mercy before I knew I'd need it most.

I lasted one semester at that school. All these years later, I still sift the ashes of those months behind the gates. Even now, nineteen years later, the lessons continue to unfold. What good could come of such a hollow, hopeless facility? The place had appropriately earned the crude and defamatory nickname "concentration camp," and while we were not physically starved or abused, the very opposite was true spiritually. With virtually every decision made for me, and even my worship regulated, my heart had soured toward God. I thought he'd abandoned me there and fought to keep bitterness at bay.

That Christmas I packed up my room and held my breath as I drove out the front gate. I never turned around to look back. I'd have spat at it if I could. I hated those grounds, but now? Now, I was free. Except I wasn't. With grades so low they couldn't transfer, I found myself living at home again, attending community college in an effort to blot out the negative marks that now marred my college transcript. I had stepped out in faith and fallen on my face—at least, that's what it felt like. I was left with little more than a low GPA and an empty feeling in my soul.

Switching from a private Christian school to a public liberal arts community college felt like standing in the heat of the blazing sun after nearly freezing to death in a wasteland. As my mind and heart thawed to new ideas, I rediscovered the freedom to think and choose for myself the truths to embrace. I searched hard for God; I demanded his answers for why he'd called me to such a place. Had I mistaken his direction? I couldn't remember anymore. I doubted both his call and his goodness. Despite the newfound sunshine of freedom, I wrestled through a season of disappointment and anger. It would be years before I realized that God was not as absent there as I had accused him of being. With time and distance between me and that experience, as I grew in my faith, God has shared glimpses of his purpose during that brief stint at school.

Months passed, and my grades improved dramatically, which really was no surprise since I had never been a failing student before. Still, despite this good news, I struggled to understand the purpose of that faith-shaking experience. Everything I'd ever learned about God had been put under the microscope of my new perspective, and I picked to pieces the truths I had been taught about God.

FINDING GOD AGAIN

In a thousand ways he continued to reveal his goodness to me. Slowly, the wounds scabbed over and healed. I found a job and gained acceptance to another four-year college. I never did apply to that design school of my earlier dreams; it no longer seemed the right fit. In every way, I was starting over. Nothing happened the way I'd imagined it would as a senior in high school. The dream of living away from home had been delayed by my bitter experience, but the truth of God's mercy began to shine through.

I'd seen the depths of a graceless place and then forgotten what grace looked like. But God had not forgotten me. He had not sent me to that school as punishment, but rather for my own refinement. In the hollows of that prayer room at the end of my hall, I'd learned to seek God with a desperate hunger that I wouldn't have known anywhere else. I learned the sweet comfort of praising him, just as Paul had done while imprisoned. God repeatedly brought comforting Scripture and songs to mind while I'd hidden away down there. The truth I see now, from the outside looking in, was that God had a specific plan for my life, not to harm me, but instead to draw me in to himself. He chose this pharisaical camp as the backdrop to love me deeply in a way I hadn't known.

He revealed to me the various little ways he'd been there all along, watching over me, protecting me and providing for me— his goodness revealed in a hundred little almost-missed ways.

It's taken years of unpacking the lessons of that refining season. I've learned to forgive the graceless and have compassion on the merciless. I've embraced Christ's love and felt the deep joy that comes only by him, even when situations appear to offer none. He saved me when I sought him—because he loves me. I called out to him from the hollows of that prayer room and he proved his goodness and the truth found in Jeremiah 29:13-14:

> "You will seek me and find me when you seek me with all your heart. I will be found by you," declares the LORD, "and will bring you back from captivity. I will gather you from all the nations and places where I have banished you," declares the LORD, "and will bring you back to the place from which I carried you into exile." (NIV 1984)

THE ROOT

Angie Hong

THE CONCERT RAN LATE and I knew I was breaking curfew, which spoiled any of the fun I had in the previous hours that night. I carefully tiptoed up to my room hoping that, for a change, my mother had already gone to sleep so my punishment would come in the morning. This wasn't the best move to make right before leaving for college. But I wasn't running too late; maybe there was a chance that she would forget about it. Maybe not.

I quietly turned the corner to enter my room, and my jaw dropped in horror as I found all my belongings in a big pile in the middle of the floor. Everything, from pencils to underwear to my computer, was built into a giant mountain. She was wild-eyed and furious, waiting for me to arrive, and like a lion pouncing on its prey she proceeded to yell and scream, reiterating her analysis that I was inherently bad. This sort of dramatic reaction to my disobedience was not unusual, each time leaving me in a state of confusion and shame. But something about the way she said it this day was different. Along with the usual berating of my character and how I would amount to nothing, I heard something different in her voice as her rage subsided. Her eyes, full of fury, now went stone cold with a look of resignation. She carefully said, "I will never trust you. I don't believe in you anymore. I give up." As our eyes met in that moment, her cold gaze penetrated the depths of my soul. My inner-fighter voice that usually said, "But I will prove you wrong," was replaced with final defeat and a laying down of arms. Suddenly overwhelmed by the wave of darkness, my mom and I wept bitterly into the night. I could not hate myself any more in that moment.

I never understood all the complicated dynamics that existed between my mom and me. There was the usual mother-daughter dynamic that so many experience: the mother as the scientist, always examining the daughter specimen and constantly tweaking in order to prime and perfect for marriage and mother-hood. I can only imagine her struggle of survival in America as a Korean immigrant, sacrificing her own wants and needs for her children and showing love in the ways that fit her culture but didn't speak to me growing up in America. But then there seemed to be an extra layer of complication that seeped into our interactions and went above and beyond these other factors. Was it okay that she tore up my favorite outfits in front of me because I wore them too much? Did it seem necessary to tear the ribbon out of my favorite cassette tape because I danced to it? Could it be right to punish me by keeping me home from school and making me hold my hands in the air all day, naked? Even now I struggle with labeling it as abuse or manipulation since this was what I thought love was.

The seed of darkness from that fateful night took root in my soul, and it had a voracious appetite. The darkness fed on shame and self-hatred so each attempt to shine and smile prettily through hurt and pain was delicious to the darkness. Busying myself with projects and jobs and tasks were delectable treats. Each coping mechanism for survival as a worthless person was a tasty meal for this darkness, and it grew and grew, flirting dangerously with any of the true parts of myself. In turn, the darkness kept me alive in a half-existence by finding more places in my soul for me to bury the pain, all of which led to deeper roots for the darkness itself. It was an ecosystem of death, one I started to feel strangely at home in.

Many years later, I rocked my newborn baby Hudson during his first days of life. I stroked his perfect little fingers and chubby cheeks. There wasn't a more perfect and innocent creature that existed on earth. I leaned in and whispered, "I love you so, so much. I will never, ever, ever . . ." and felt the tears well up in anguish as the painful memories of that night of resignation came to the surface. I wanted to say, "I will never make you feel like a waste of a space." I wanted to say, "I will never make you feel rejected or ashamed of who you are." I really wanted to say those things to my precious baby in full confidence. But I couldn't bring myself to finish that sentence because I couldn't know for sure if it was true. I couldn't say that I had broken the cycle of abuse and violence simply by avoiding the pain of the past and living in survival mode. But somehow I knew that there was some active work to be done, a deep healing, and God was beckoning me to it now more than ever.

How does one begin unraveling the wounds of the past? I had grown quite accustomed to this dark ecosystem. It was my

modus operandi, my shelter, my hiding place. It had gotten me
this far, right? There were times when I let the darkness take over
me as I numbly handed over the controls, resulting in some
roadblocks. But then I always seemed to recover and hide my
tracks somewhat well. It didn't seem so bad. Plus, I was completely terrified of what I would uncover once I began, deathly
afraid of feeling the lifetime of pain I had tried so hard to
conceal. I didn't even know how to approach God in an honest
way. Surely the God of the universe didn't have time to deal with
my silly thoughts and desires. They weren't worth bringing as an
offering. I wasn't worthy. I felt like Adam and Eve, using puny
little leaves to cover myself when God knew all along who I was
and exactly what I was doing.

And yet I heard God's still, small voice, so strong yet so
peaceful, saying, "I want more. Bring it all to me. All of it."

At first, I enlisted the help of a professional therapist because
I knew I couldn't do it alone. This moved me light years ahead
in terms of confronting the pain. It felt powerful to name my
shame and counter it with truth that revealed a little more of
who I really was, who I was created to be. That active and fa-
cilitated work provided me the tools and courage to go at it
work by myself in the everyday quiet moments. One tip I received from a friend was to allow myself three pages every
morning to write down everything going on in my heart and
soul as a concrete offering to God. I began writing everything
down in its raw form, unpolished and unattractive, sometimes
even spilling beyond the allotted three pages. At first I was half
expecting some sort of punishment from God, or even a sign of
resignation similar to my mother's. No doubt it was exhausting
to hear. But God received every word, fear, anxiety and even

silliness with arms wide open. There was a tenderness I felt, as if God actually treasured every word written, even celebrated it. It was unchartered territory, and as I took each step of discovery I was being swallowed up in the quicksand of God's unending love and mercy. I was free falling, all the way down until I hit the most solid and sure ground I had ever known—the ground that was there all along.

As much as I was tempted to banish the darkness or pretend it wasn't there anymore, I realized that hiding it would lead to shame, thus reigniting the vicious ecosystem. Instead, I fed the darkness with hope and love, the same hope and love that had been gifted to me in abundance as I stood taller and taller in my nakedness before God. I fed it creativity and compassion, and kindly made room for the darkness to be redeemed in the light of the living God. I included the story of the darkness, thanking it for giving me an extra layer of depth and texture that could hopefully be a gift to others someday. That dark root that had been planted so many years ago was morphing into a thriving hybrid plant, flourishing wildly in its complexity and wholeness.

> Instead of the thorn bush will grow the juniper,
> and instead of the briers the myrtle will grow.
> This will be for the LORD's renown,
> for an everlasting sign,
> that will endure forever. (Is 55:13)

Revealing every little nook and cranny of ourselves to God is terrifying, and yet also extremely exhilarating. Admitting that we need help in the free fall to authenticity comes from a place of awareness and wisdom, never from a place of weakness. We can learn to see ourselves as God sees us, and to sort out the distorted views that have been so deeply ingrained and rooted in our souls. And God, ever faithful, joyfully forges our path the whole way.

THE WAGING
AND THE WAITING

Tammy Perlmutter

IN 1977, MY MOTHER LEFT my brothers and me with sitters to go looking for an apartment and didn't return for days. When she finally did, after what most people considered a "lost weekend," my brother and I were placed in foster care. I was not quite five. It *was* a lost weekend, because *I lost everything*— my home, my family and what little sense of stability an alcoholic parent could provide. I also lost my history. I remember so little I can't even get a gut-wrenching, soul-crushing memoir out of the train wreck of my life. I've battled depression and anxiety ever since.

For years, when I spoke of that event, the lost weekend, I always said, "We were taken away from my mom when I was four." That's only partly true. This is the first time I've called it what it really was. "My mom *left me* when I was four." There wasn't an unknown *they*. The *man*. The *system*. For thirty years I believed that my family had little to do with my being "taken away." Then one Thanksgiving, reunited with my brother David, the truth came out.

"It was Granny and Aunt Pinky that called DCFS on us." Silence. Cogs whirring. Memories scanned. All these years I believed we were "taken away" from family, and what really happened is that we were "given up" by family? There is no way to describe that feeling, the uncovering of that truth.

This wasn't a passive relinquishment of two children. This was an active participation in the *giving up* of two children.

My mother was given a choice between her addiction and her children. The ugly, painful truth is that she chose her addiction, year after year. She chose her addiction over being a mother, and over monthly visits with her children. My mother was a victim too. But I believed she was going to be the hero one day. She was going to come back for me. We were going to live together again, and Elvis Presley was going to be my dad.

It's funny now. And sad. The only thing I knew about my mother was that she loved Elvis. I didn't know her favorite color or her favorite flower. In my fantasy, we all got what we wanted. My mom got Elvis and I got her, and we lived happily ever after.

In all, there were five foster homes, eight schools, one group home, one children's home, one physically and emotionally abusive home, two sexually abusive homes, one perverted youth pastor who kissed me in the dark church, two predatory teachers, one father who I knew briefly as an infant, one brother who ran away so much we were separated, and one mother who could rarely be found or bother to show up for a monthly parental visit.

After the third or fourth or ninth time my mother failed to show up for her visitation, I figured it out. There was no truth to my fantasy. It was never going to happen. I was always going to be the girl whose mother didn't love her enough to keep her, the girl who wasn't even worth her mother's love. The disposable, invisible, expendable little girl who had no worth even to the woman who gave birth to her.

There was never a time I didn't see myself like that. Even in the good foster home, I never felt like I belonged or like I was claimed as anyone's. The different last names, my blonde hair and blue eyes setting me apart from the darker-eyed families I was placed with. My early loss defined me and set me apart. There was no way to pretend it didn't.

The loneliness was excruciating. There was no one to talk to. The social workers alternated all the time. I didn't have enough of "me" to believe my opinion mattered or could be expressed so I told them what they wanted to hear. I smiled and nodded. I packed up my clothes.

I longed for a home. What I got was a stranger's house for undetermined amounts of time with monthly visits to the grandmother, aunt and cousins who were privileged to live together while I lived apart. Nothing was ever "real" for me. I was never one of the "real" kids, and I never lived with my "real" family. I was so unknown. I didn't know how to speak up, to ask for what I wanted or needed. I didn't know how to tell them I preferred one thing over another so I made myself small. I wanted to disappear altogether.

Even as I got older there weren't many memories I could go back to. Truthfully, they are most likely blocked for a reason. I saw faces, houses, scenes I couldn't tell were real. But what I do remember are the nights. The sleepless, achingly lonely nights when I cried and cried until my sobs rocked me to sleep. The nights I put my own hands around my throat and choked myself into unconsciousness, hoping that would be the fatal one. I remember the knives and razor blades and scissors, the over-the-counter pills I stole trying to find the deadly dose and getting so drunk I blacked out and ended up on a stranger's lawn.

There were required weekly therapist visits from third grade on. There was a two-week stay on a psych unit when I was seventeen where I confessed my deepest, darkest shame: being molested at ten. I couldn't speak the words out loud so I wrote them on a piece of paper and gave them to Lori as I was leaving. Group therapy was suggested. Seriously? For a girl who can't speak the words out loud behind a closed door to one person? The matter was dropped, but only on their end. It never ended for me.

There was medication. More counseling. The children's home. College. Wandering. Vandalism. Theft. More drinking. More risky behavior, hoping that something would just *happen* to me that would end it all. I had nowhere to go until a friend helped me get to a residential ministry in Chicago where misfits, outcasts, and lost and lonely people could find a home, a church and a purpose. I did find all of those things and more. I found family, a husband, a calling.

I discovered my gifts for mentoring and discipleship. I was given space and encouragement to write, publishing articles and poetry for *Cornerstone* magazine. I had the privilege of meeting musicians like Over the Rhine, Victoria Williams, Maria McKee and Julie Miller. I met some favorite authors too: Kathleen Norris, Luci Shaw, Lauren Winner, Irina Ratushinskaya, Doris Betts. I spoke to Anne Lamott on the floor of the gym at Calvin College. I sat at Henri Nouwen's feet when he spoke about drinking the cup. I read *original* letters by C. S.

Lewis in the Wade Center at Wheaton College and assisted in publishing several books on Lewis, MacDonald, Tolkien and Flannery O'Connor.

All of these experiences were life changing, and the people I shared my life with were extraordinary in countless ways. My husband and daughter still make my heart beat faster. God has been faithful and loving and merciful to me with such abandon that it makes me ashamed to admit that I still have that darkness inside me.

After all the years, all the counseling, all the forgiving, all the medication, all the agonizing authenticity and cringing confessions, I still get gloomy. After the diagnoses of major depression, anxiety and PTSD, I still get weepy when the sun starts to sink below the horizon. I still lie awake at night with panic from events and conversations of the day and memories and nightmares from the past.

The last two years have been the longest, bloodiest battles against my own shadowy heart and hopeless spirit I've ever known. There was so much against us—church conflict, deaths, job loss, parenting defeats, destruction of community, financial ruin, health problems.

It was the middle of February last year, recovering from emergency surgery and the demise of a friendship, when I first told my husband I was struggling with suicidal thoughts. There was just no light in our future. I was so tired, so deeply hurt, so desperately disappointed. But I hung on.

Life didn't magically improve in the hanging on, it only grew blacker and sharper and more suffocating. Eight months later it was so much worse. For weeks on end I was waking up praying that it was a nightmare, that I was really dead and being alive was the dream. I didn't know who to share this with, how to present the subject, or how not to draw a person in with my candidness and simultaneously repel them with my darkness.

In September I got scared. The temptation to cut reared its bloody head again. It was all I could think about. If I couldn't kill myself, then I should at least be able to cut. The thoughts of cutting and dying were becoming fantasies, and I entertained them longer and more frequently. Something had to be done. I needed help. More help.

One morning I told my husband that I loved him and I loved my daughter, Phoenix, and I would never want to hurt them in any way, but this black, gaping, hungry hole in the middle of my soul was taking over the rest of me, and I just wanted to jump in and be done.

Mike listened. Then he prayed for me and over me. While I was slumped over and crying and hopeless and terrified, he prayed blessing, deliverance, wholeness and protection over my heart, my mind and my body.

And God answered. Though I doubted in the midst of his prayer, God heard and moved. And this time, for whatever reason, he moved almost immediately. I felt relieved in sharing this burden, the panic lessened and I could breathe deeply again. The darkness seemed to recede, and I noticed a buoyancy of spirit filling me.

For me, hope wasn't a thing of feathers. The tendrils wound around my heart as he prayed, and I felt my heart begin to beat with a different cadence, not the slow, irregular plodding of despair but the steady pulse of solace. My breathing slowed, and somewhere inside, where there had been only darkness and chaos, there was now a little more light.

God acknowledged every pain and ache and wound, and he heard me. While I was driven to distraction with the desire to end the life he gave me, he delivered me, healed me and rejoiced over me with singing. He quieted me with his love. He *rescued* me.

That was four months ago. From that moment, when my husband stormed the gates of hell for my soul, the thoughts, the fantasies and the temptations to cut and to die vanished. I was released. I haven't felt the same way since, and instead, I have peace and joy I never thought possible and would have scoffed about before.

I believe God delivered me that day through the fervent prayer of a righteous man who was willing to wage war for his wife's soul. This freedom and hope I feel is supernatural in the most divine sense. The hurting was years in the making, and the healing was years in the happening, but it *did* happen and it will continue, this already and also not yet. The difference is, I can wait for the not yet. I'm not going to take it by force. I'm going to let it be sung over me, and the song will be sweeter for the waiting.

THE YEARBOOK

Linda Basmeson

IN 1999, RICKY MARTIN was reminding us to live the "vida loca," and Britney Spears was at the top of the pop charts. And I, too, was at the top of my game—juggling advanced classes, extracurricular activities and a part-time job. That was the year I was voted "most dependable" by my fellow high school seniors. I was excited to have my picture in the yearbook next to such an honorary title. This was a title I could put on my college applications to Stanford and Yale.

But as my senior year progressed, I became anything but dependable. I was stretched to my limit in terms of time and energy. My grades suffered, my friendships waned, and worst of all, I got involved with the wrong guy and became another teen pregnancy statistic. I had let myself and my family down; I was a phony.

The enemy of my soul had gotten his way. He was able to poignantly target my weakest points. I wanted approval, and he gave me a cameo in the yearbook. I wanted to be successful, and

he gave me a full schedule that never made room for God, family
or friends. I wanted to be loved for who I was; instead he gave
me sex disguised as unconditional acceptance.

As a child, I was convinced I was a mistake. I had been raised
by a single mother who had put aside her dreams of going to a
prestigious school in Los Angeles to work full time and care for
me. My father was an auto mechanic who I met only once or
twice. The few times he wrote to me were from his jail cell. He
told me he would come back to see me; instead he died young
of apparent "natural causes." It is hard to disentangle from a
family legacy like that, but I had been determined to "rise above"
these circumstances.

Instead, as the years went by I saw my entire life as one huge
failure. I was a single mother always trying to make ends meet
and my relationship with God was driven by an inner desire to
undo my past wrongs. I became legalistic, fearful and joyless. I
had failed him and was not the daughter he could depend on. I
was just a fraction of what I could have become had I truly been
what the pages of that yearbook said I was.

I would often go back to those pages and mentally rewrite
my superlative: "most likely to get pregnant by age 19," "most
likely to *not* live up to her potential," "most likely to be constantly stressed and tired," "most likely to yell at her kids over
small slip-ups because of overwhelming anger toward herself."
If anyone had shown up in those moments and said otherwise,
I would have slapped them with a bullet-pointed list of my
life's failures.

The fear of rejection drove almost everything I did. I gravi-
tated toward acceptance, whether it was good or bad. I dated
men who treated me poorly or were less than God's ultimate

best for me. I worked at jobs that were draining and lackluster. I was fearful of stepping out in faith to do what I really dreamed of doing because I was relying on the current man in my life or the job on my résumé to be my safety net.

I was only in my early twenties but was already experiencing a second adolescence. Every time I picked up a Bible I turned to the same verses:

> Consider it pure joy, my brothers and sisters, whenever you face trials of many kinds, because you know that the testing of your faith produces perseverance. Let perseverance finish its work so that you may be mature and complete, not lacking anything. If any of you lacks wisdom, you should ask God, who gives generously to all without finding fault, and it will be given to you. But when you ask, you must believe and not doubt, because the one who doubts is like a wave of the sea, blown and tossed by the wind. (Jas 1:2-6)

One night I dreamt I was on a yacht. A storm had rolled in, tossing and tilting that mighty vessel. I could only hang on and hope that God would calm the winds. I felt helpless and afraid. I woke up sweating and more worn out than when I had gone to bed. The dream was so vividly real. That is when I heard for the first time the undeniable voice of God: "Linda, if you do not obey me and continue to doubt, you will be like that boat— tossed by the wind and raging sea!"

I realized in that moment that I had kept myself busy. By making my own life complicated, I had ignored the quiet stillness that I thought would lead to despair. I had expected so much of myself, when all Jesus wanted was my heart. I surrendered my lonely, trampled heart that had long been numb . . . and found my new love. Jesus Christ met me where my pride and arrogance ended. He knew I doubted his love for me and had instead tried to earn it. He gently reminded me of truths long forgotten.

His love was visible. "We love him, because he first loved us" (1 Jn 4:19 KJV). He was not ashamed of me because there is no fear in love.

His love was committed. He saw my sin but wanted to walk me through the restorative process. His love would not run out or grow cold.

His love was unconditional. Not only did he not hold my sins against me but he also did not require me to undo my past before wrapping his loving arms around me. He did not ask me to worry. He did not ask me to work harder. He just invited me to sit at his feet.

His love was sacrificial. He kept his promises to me even in the midst of my inward wonderings. He was faithful, patient and kind. He ran to meet his prodigal daughter and covered my sins with his sacrifice on the cross.

His love was healing. His forgiveness allowed me to forgive myself. His Spirit filled me and comforted me.

There was a deeper work that needed to be done, and it began that moment in my room. There are still moments where I struggle with unworthiness and fear. Christ brings me back to the place where my real relationship began with him: on the floor of my bedroom with an open Bible. Somehow the cold, hard floor of my bedroom had turned from a place where I mourned lost dreams into a place where I found hope for a restored future.

In the years that followed I still met men that were not God's best for me, but they no longer controlled my weary, desperate, lonely heart. Now I have hope that Jesus is preparing a mate who will have a committed, visible, sacrificial love toward me.

I still struggle with contentment in my job, but I have found hope in knowing that Christ has gone before me and will continue to lead me like a gentleman. Everything that I do is for him, and he alone is my promoter.

Most important, I have grown to understand that God's grace is truly sufficient. Those broken places in my heart have been made whole by Jesus. Like the potter and the clay, his hands are able to transform a marred vessel into something useful. Nothing is lost.

I recently thumbed through the pages of my yearbook with new eyes. I saw hope in those captions. My eyes did not see a woman who had not lived up to her potential but instead a woman Christ paid the ultimate sacrifice for. I no longer see myself in those pages; I see him. I see his timing, his purpose and his plan unfold even in the midst of the darkest hours of my life.

So I rewrote the superlative: "Only Jesus Is 'Most Dependable.'" What a relief to know that his love is not determined by our dependability but on his faithfulness! I still struggle to juggle commitments. I more often seek approval from those around me instead of from God. I still lean too much on my own understanding and find myself overwhelmed. In the midst of my mess and my imperfections, one thing remains: he loves me; I am not a failure in his eyes. I can be vulnerable about my struggles because his love for me made him vulnerable. I am free to live life candidly because his power is made perfect in my weakness. He rewrites my superlative on the pages of Scripture

where I find the truth that defines who I really am: loved, redeemed and rescued. Instead of dependable, I find myself utterly
dependent on him for every need.

OF OLD MIRRORS
AND NEW DOORS

Kelli Woodford

THE PAST CAME KNOCKING TODAY. I was preparing for a baby
shower on Saturday. Each attendee was requested to bring a
photo of herself with her firstborn child. I sort through picture
albums in the basement, looking for a photo of me at twenty-
three, still young enough to be brazen and opinionated, holding
my firstborn. Carefully sorting through fragile moments and
tender places, I also avoid spider webs and keep an eye open for
other unwanted visitors.

I know that in places undisturbed, sometimes things can take
up residence. And there, in the midst of the old newspaper clip-
pings and 35-millimeter negatives, I run across something I
wasn't looking for.

My hand searches in the box for the yellow album with a
smiling, rosy-cheeked Noah enjoying his ark and his animal
friends, but—*how could I know?*—the Searcher of hearts was
uncovering too. And his hand reached deep in *me*.

Because how would I choose which picture to take—which sweet blue bundle in my fumbling arms—when I have *two* *firstborns?* When I've faltered under the weight of inexperience *twice?*

I pick out the one where my hair is curled and bleach-blond, leaning on a black futon, firstborn number two in my arms. Nice picture. Nice and safe.

I look long at it, and almost eleven years pass before my mind's eye. Years of pacifiers and peek-a-boo have slowly crept into years of inline skates and fishing trips. And I've been there for all of it. A satisfied sigh escapes my lips, but something within me turns. *What about that other box? The other album, the one kept up on a high shelf for all these seventeen years? Why don't I take out a picture of my real firstborn?*

Slowly, learning to be led by that quiet whisper that never steers me wrong, I pull down the box.

This one is dustier. Messier.

My heart pounds, an old wound reopening. As I leaf through aged photo albums and yellowing letters, I settle on a picture.

Far from old enough to be brazen and opinionated, I am in pink corduroy and my sixteen years look innocently out of place, holding my *real* firstborn. *Is it possible that I was so young looking when he was born?*

Oh, I remember the feeling of inexperience. I remember the way I felt so unprepared for labor and delivery—even after attending all the classes with my mother at my side. How I just decided to trust God, and that the hardest part wasn't the long labor or the pitocin drip or the forceps.

The hardest part came three days later when I signed away my rights to parent this child.

Placing him in the arms of a woman I had chosen to be his mother through careful examination of photo after photo, letter after letter. *And not taking him back.*

I brush dust off the album and resist the temptation to run from this. This is not safe. But this is part of me, and I must relive it.

That third day, kissing his perfect forehead and weeping. Learning that love doesn't always mean holding on; sometimes, *to really love, you have to let go.*

Seventeen years, and my tears of today mingle with those of the young lady in the picture. The one who seems so fragile now. Long ago and far away. Locked up in a box on the top shelf all these years, the one who still holds him in her timid arms. Returning to the wound has been hard, and I wonder, *did I ever really let go?*

All the years, their memories stacked up to the top of the box, when I would check the mail like my life depended on it, just for a card, a note, a picture . . . something. Just for a way to hold on a little longer.

She had been a good mom, and she sent me detailed letters, every one of them tucked safely away in the box. Photos, locks of hair, traced hands and feet—you name it. I treasured these. And I began to heal.

But only slowly, in the seventeen years passing, did I also begin to hide.

Hiding is impossible at first. A sixteen-year-old pregnant girl gets stuck in the desks in geometry class, leans against the wall alone in youth group, and endures raised eyebrows and clucking tongues at her fast-food job. I wore shame like a red letter.

But as he turned one and broke teeth through his gums, I looked through college recruitment papers and got ready to take the ACT. And no one there seemed to notice that shame so much anymore. The crimson was fading. And just before he turned three, I started my first semester at college.

Lumped in with the all the other freshmen, I saw my chance to start over. To hide what I had done. To wear anything but that red letter. So I put on a mask instead and I learned the art of *faking*.

I got so good at it that it continued through four years of Bible college, an inner-city missions job and eight years as a pastor's wife before I finally realized that the wound underneath all my layers was festering, and it wouldn't heal in the dark.

Still trembling with the power of memory, I hold my two pictures in hand and take them upstairs. It's lighter there.

The floor still needs to be vacuumed, so I begin to unwind the cord. Slowly, it all comes out.

I know that the way to fellowship with God is in the light and not the dark, so I pray as I weave back and forth over the pencil shavings that litter the carpet, asking for his eyes to see to the bottom of this deep water, this dark well.

How can I still be so moved by the pain of a choice I made almost two decades ago? And what does it mean to really "let go"? Why is it so ridiculously hard to decide which picture to take to the shower?

The phrase that I sense over my whirring Kirby is like a balm: *Know and be known.*

And I think I know what he means.

I have *known* many dark secrets and can tell names and places of people who have entrusted me with their hearts. From the late nights in the dorm to the heart-breaking counseling sessions and the testimonies that dare to bare it all, many people have let me *know* them.

But have I been known?

Do I even know myself?

When do skeletons in the closet actually hold the closet door closed so tight that you can't breathe in there? How do undisturbed places grow to have a life of their own? And how did I get trapped in this prison, created so I wouldn't have to wear shame anymore? It seemed a safe enough place to hide.

Dark. Undisturbed. Like a grave.

Maybe it is time. And maybe I could be Lazarus and come forth by this word, this *knowing and being known.*

Could this be the way to really "let go" of the past, the past I thought I was holding but have finally realized *it's holding onto me?* To bring it *into the light* of the present?

No more hiding. No more holding on. No more shameful letters.

The time has come to stop being frightened by the face in the mirror and unlock that young lady from the picture.

She is me and I am her.

And I will not deny any longer. I will learn to forgive. *Forgive myself.*

If I just but taste his forgiveness and perfect love—*knowing and being completely known by God*—it paves the vulnerable way with courage for me to let go of the secret so I can know and be known by others. It paves the vulnerable way with courage for me to accept myself, in the light of his love.

Resurrection. Light. A new life, *unafraid,* awaits.

I walk through the open door.

Part Two

LEANING IN

LIQUID COURAGE

Amy Smith

WAS DRUNK AT CHURCH.

I hadn't meant to be.

I was lonely, struggling to make friends, searching for God in the faces of the women in my Bible study. It had been awhile since I had tried to connect to anyone inside of a church.

They were lovely, with their designer clothes and stylish haircuts and perfectly manicured fingernails. In some ways, I fit right in. For starters, I was white. I had never been to a church before where there were so many white people. I found it strangely unsettling.

They all knew each other, and while they were cordial—friendly, even—I knew they all wanted to sit with their friends, and that did not leave space for me. Who wants to be a third wheel? I was stunned to find that church, just like high school, was bereft with cliques. The feeling of passive rejection stung.

I didn't belong here. I had assumed it would be like this—me sitting with my head slightly down, my body language screaming with emotional fragility, trying to avoid eye contact lest anyone should notice me and give a smile of pity.

I was right.

So before I got in my car and drove to the church, I'd decided I needed a little liquid courage.

I took a shot of rum before I left.

But when that did not seem to be kicking in nearly quick enough, I took a couple more. I don't remember how many I had. I lost count after the fourth. The warmth traveled down, down, down. The tight knot in my stomach began to unwind, my shoulders began to relax. My hands stopped shaking. I looked at myself in the mirror and thought: *Yes. I can do this.*

I applied more mascara with steady hands.

I don't know why it was so important for me to go to that meeting. I only know I was searching for Jesus and thought he might be there.

I did okay until I sat down at that table. I started to glaze over, and I'm pretty sure I was swaying in my seat.

I flew.

With wild, crazed eyes and a strong shot of panic when the sensation hit me, I flew.

I barely made it out the door.

I vomited up the contents of my stomach. There wasn't much there, really, because I had all but stopped eating.

Some folks eat when they are stressed. Not me. When I am stressed, I can barely eat at all.

A couple of ladies rushed out to help and I blurted out the first lie I could think of to cover my shame. I told them I thought I was pregnant. Then I started to cry, humiliated. One of the ladies offered to drive me home. I sat in her car, the world spinning, thoughts of self-loathing threatening to overtake me. What kind of a loser goes to church drunk?

Groaning from the headache that was starting to form at the base of my neck, I stumbled out of the car and into my husband's arms. He helped me get into the bathtub. I was bawling. Tears rolled hot down my cheeks and made plunking noises as they hit the bath water.

Did God really collect all these mascara-tinged, pathetic tears in some sort of bottle, as the Psalms said?

The kind woman who brought me home drove my husband back to the church to get our car. I remember wanting to sink beneath the sudsy water in that tub, longing just to drift away. I tried to will myself to drown, to close my eyes and heart for good, to embrace oblivion once and for all, but I couldn't. Instead, I made hysterical phone calls to several of my friends. I didn't tell them I had been drinking. I just told them I was sick. It wasn't entirely a lie.

Eventually, my husband got back and helped me to bed. The room was spinning faster and faster out of control. I don't know how long it took but I finally started to dream, little bits of my subconscious taunting and mocking me. They were sad dreams that made no sense. Like Alice, trying to find her way out of Wonderland, I slept it off.

It wasn't until I woke up in the morning with a massive hangover, disgusted with myself, that I heard him speak—soft and gentle and dripping with love and hope for his soul-sick girl.

At first, I didn't believe it was him. I believed you had to get your life all cleaned up, tidy and holy and good before he would speak to you. I wondered whether God really spoke to people at all these days. Wasn't he distant, far away and uninterested, watching with only mild interest the goings-on of his so-called creation? I assumed that if he spoke at all it was to important, spiritual people like ascetics and mystics and the pope and maybe Billy Graham, but definitely not to broken, sinful, jacked-up people like me.

But he did.

Against all odds, with a pounding headache and a cup of strong, hot coffee warming my hands, I heard him whisper a single word.

Grace.

And to be honest, it scared the hell out of me.

I grew up in church, though sometime in my teens I rejected it because I saw so much hypocrisy it turned my stomach. I was tired of hearing people claim God as their own personal genie. I was sick of sensing that only a thin veil covered what was really there—people who said they were Christians but who I was embarrassed to associate myself with. I had friends in high school who told me they thought my church was a cult and loved me anyway. But my "friends" in church insisted that I get rid of any friends who weren't Christians, that I shouldn't socialize with people outside of church, that I shouldn't go to my prom or other school functions, and that I shouldn't dance.

I was sick to death of hearing people use grace as an excuse to be evil, to cover up their sin and to use repugnant clichés like "God isn't finished with me yet," and "I'm not perfect, just forgiven." I was sick of grace because it had lost its meaning. It felt cheap, and it carried no weight or value in my heart. I saw grace as nothing more than a subterfuge, a justification for bad behavior, a thinly veiled disguise wrapped up in the language of Christianese.

And yet, that was the word I heard that morning as I debated whether I'd be able to hold down food.

Grace?

It's strange how years of studying Buddhism and trying to be zen—to be at peace—had jaded me. I'd tried using the principles of feng shui to bring tranquility to my personal spaces, but inside I was raging, hungry and aching. I was still searching.

I pulled out the old Maranatha records I grew up with and just listened awhile as I got dressed and went through my quotidian routine. The grace he whispered into my ear started to seep down into the parched, impoverished, exhausted recesses of my heart. I was reminded of something I'd once known.

Peace is a person.

I knew in an instant what I'd been confused about for years. He loved me. I didn't have to pretend to be someone else, and I didn't really *need* other people to love and accept me. I didn't have to put on a mask every time I walked out my door. I didn't have to say yes to every request or work myself bone-weary to impress. I didn't need Captain Morgan to be brave, calm or fun.

I am sometimes asked when I was "saved"—when my spiritual conversion took place. The short answer is: I don't remember. I don't remember my physical birth either, but I know it took place because I am alive. Spiritually, it is much the same. I can't give you the date, and sometimes it feels like it happened in degrees, gradually and not instantaneously. I'll bet that rattles some folks' doctrine a little, but it's true.

I was a little more saved after that. When I first took a headlong plunge into the deep waters of grace, a metamorphosis began. It was when, like a newly delivered child gasping for that first lung-searing breath, I began to come alive.

JOY TO THE WORLD! REALLY? WHERE?

Deana Chadwell

WE RECALL THE ANGELIC announcement at Christ's birth, "And the angel said unto them, Fear not: for, behold, I bring you good tidings of great joy, which shall be to all people" (Lk 2:10 KJV). But almost two thousand years later I often hear people scoff at this verse, and for good reason. The "great tidings" have taken second chair to news alerts, and rarely are those joyful. So, was the angel just blowing smoke? Where is all this joy?

Here—everywhere—but under the radar, in unexpected places. Not anywhere near a winning lottery ticket or a new house or the shedding of fifty pounds. Of course, I'd not refuse those things, but I don't expect joy to come with them. Joy is already present. Yesterday joy wore lavender flannel PJs, sat on my lap and read me poetry, the lovely words riding her animated little voice, all light and lyrical. Today joy hovers around the wood stove where some old oak radiates warmth just a few feet from the snow outside. Joy rises like steam from a bowl of soup, flashes at us from the iridescent neon of a hummingbird's head, fills our lungs with blue sky. The stuff it is made of surrounds us, indwells us and costs us nothing.

Joy even follows us into the dark valleys. When my husband was diagnosed with cancer three years ago our whole world went black. I did my usual research and more research, arming myself with every fact I could locate. That helped equip me for our fights with the medical community, but little by little I started to see God's hand in all of it, and with that realization joy arrived. It came in amazing, unexpected ways: the exhausting day we found—against all odds—two painters who helped us finish painting some high and dangerous gables; the day we actually got an appointment with a nationally known surgeon and our first meeting with him and his quiet careful optimism and assurance; the evening I met three women whom I suspect were angels.

When I look back on that time now I mostly remember color, not blackness. The waiting room paintings are still etched in my mind—a triptych featuring a half-dozen couples standing in various parts of a garden, all in jewel tones and gilded. It caught the early morning light and wrapped me in its beauty. I remember the life-size crimson horse in the vestibule of the surgical wing, the framed silk kimonos, the "moat" of blue sea glass at the base of the sweeping stairs. When the surgery was finally over and they took Tom to his room I stood in awe at the view from his bed. He could look out over the University of Washington campus in fall colors, across the canal and fairytale drawbridge toward Lake Washington. Mount Rainier posed in the background, snow-swathed and regal. All that beauty soothed my anxieties and covered us both with God's obvious care.

While Tom recovered we stayed in a small inn on the campus; its front awning and carriage lanterns matched the red of the pin oaks on the curb. It sat at the bottom of a hill. At the top of that hill was a charming coffee house—all chocolate brown and cozy. A couple of blocks farther on stood the campus Trader Joe's filled with brightly colored produce and backpacked students. Odd, but I remember our few days in that inn very fondly. There was joy there.

There was even joy the day I drove Tom home—seven hours in lashing rain, rain so dense I could hardly see, and as we slogged through Portland, the water was high enough that it sloshed its way into the trunk. As cars passed on lanes above us, whole walls of water whacked the windshield and blinded me. My knuckles went white and my shoulders knotted, but then a miracle happened—the clouds cleared and a brilliant rainbow appeared. Instant color against all that gray, and it lasted just long enough for me to notice it. The rain returned, but I got the message, and joy was with us because God was with us. All was under his control. I had needed that reminder and in his love, he gave it to me.

Joy does not have to be muffled in the monotonous. Joy is *in* the mundane, in the little things, and in our determination to notice them. God has graciously filled this world with wonder, and I don't mean the Grand Canyon or flights to the moon, but all the amazements in our day-to-day lives—if we choose to notice. In *Our Town,* playwright Thornton Wilder has his heroine, Emily Webb, who has just died in childbirth, revisit a day in her life. She chooses her twelfth birthday but then finds the experience terribly disturbing. She understands how much she missed. She asks the Stage Manager—the "narrator" of the story—if anyone ever "realizes life while they live it?—every, every minute." He answers, "No. Saints and poets maybe . . . they do some." Then Emily gives us a list of the things she failed to appreciate while she was alive. She says,

> Good-by, good-by world. Good-by, Grover's Corners . . .
> Mama and Papa. Good-by to clocks ticking . . . and Mama's
> sunflowers. And food and coffee. And new-ironed dresses,
> and hot baths . . . and sleeping and waking up. Oh, earth,
> you're too wonderful for anyone to realize you.

Delight is in those small, inconsequential things. We just have to turn up our joy detector, notice and give credit to the God who provided them. Joy is in our gratitude.

Ken Macrorie, who has written some of my favorite books on teaching writing, had his students keep journals in which they recorded tiny events or observations embedded with irony or surprise, heavy with unexpected beauty or weighty with meaning. There was a time when I would have barely glanced at the bearded man riding his bike through the Safeway parking lot, his parrot perched confidently on his shoulder. Before I learned to pay attention, the guy in the doctor's office parking lot might not have made an impression. There I was waiting, bored and impatient. I couldn't concentrate on my book, the magazine rack only held someone's leftover *Golf Digest*, and people watching requires more than two elderly men. Then, clip-clop, clip-clop, and through the plate-glass window I watched a cowboy—ten-gallon hat and a huge silver belt-buckle—"parking" his caramel and white pinto. He dismounted, flipped the reins over the pommel, patted the horse's muzzle and walked into the building. I snuck a glance at the two old guys to see if they'd seen it too. Raised eyebrows and head shakes told me they had and that I wasn't nuts. I was no longer bored—I've been happily reliving that little incident for years.

But how did I learn to pay appreciative attention to the world outside of myself? It didn't, and doesn't, come naturally. I learned in fits and starts in spite of the fact that the lessons were coming at me from all directions. I picked up some of it from taking watercolor lessons the fall my youngest grandson died. Concentrating on mixing exactly the right burgundies to match the leaves of a red plum not only shut out the fear and grief, but it made me actually *look* at that marvelous color; God made that.

Some of this observational skill I learned in a similar manner from writing poetry—I discovered that I couldn't describe the multi-colored reflections made by headlights on wet pavement unless I closely observed them. But most of my appreciation for all the silly, splendid, particular things that surround us I learned by studying God. Remember the lines of the hymn "Turn your eyes upon Jesus / Look full in his wonderful face"? Glorious as those lyrics are, the next lines aren't quite right: "And the things of earth will grow strangely dim / In the light of his glory and grace." In my experience the "things of earth" have grown lovelier, more surprising and delightful in that light. Turn our eyes toward Jesus and everything shines—even the tough spots morph into excitement. *How is he going to solve my problem this time?* When I am consciously aware of him, life fills with wonder, and wonder brings joy.

That sounds a little too simple, and perhaps it is. By "turning my eyes upon Jesus," I've learned that this business of taking every thought into captivity for Christ (2 Cor 10:5) is my life's work and the outcome is joy—sparkling spots of wonder, of delightful surprise, of hilarity, of silliness.

God is love, justice, goodness, eternal life, sovereignty, and he is also perfect happiness. He has a sense of humor. He is joy.

NUANCE

Seth Haines

How long must I take counsel in my soul
and have sorrow in my heart all the day? . . .
But I have trusted in your steadfast love;
my heart shall rejoice in your salvation.
I will sing to the LORD,
because he has dealt bountifully with me.

PSALM 13:2, 5-6 ESV

TITUS AND I STOOD at the fifth-floor window, watching the morning rush on the highway below. "They are going to work," I say, then point to a passing car and say, "zoom, zoom." Titus smiles and points to the window too, runs his finger back and forth against the glass and mumbles "zum-a-zum-a-zum-a." There are two women at the nurse's station behind us. One sits at the desk in scrubs and reviews notations on medical charts. The other—a family member of another child in the hospital—rattles on as if the nurse is listening to her. She's watching us, and when I notice, she takes it as an invitation to conversation.

"Ooh, he's tiny," she near-whispers, squinting her eyes and leaning into her words. She straightens, smiles, adds, "cute too," as if it were an apologetic afterthought. "How old is he?" she asks.

"He'll be one on Saturday."

"Lord!" she says, nearly jumping back into the nurses' station. "That boy's small!"

"I know. That's sort of why we're here."

"How much does he weigh?" She asks, and now she wears a look of put-on concern. She pulls her glasses down and peers over the top of them as if straining to get a better look.

"About as much as a small six-month old," I say.

Titus's cheek is framed by the feeding tube that runs up his nose and down into his intestines. His brown eyes are overly large against the backdrop of his diminutive frame, and he flashes them at the gawking woman before turning back to the broad window. The woman wishes me luck, turns back to her conversation with the nurse. Titus is unaware that he is the spectacle and points again to the cars hustling to work.

The woman begins to talk loudly about her grandson. He's big, she says, "ninety-fifth percentile in height and weight. His mama was asking me the other day what ball we should use in his one-year portraits. She said 'soccer'? and I said, 'Now, does he look like a soccer player to you? That boy's gonna play football.'" She continues her pronouncements of grandeur—his size, his intellect, his devilish good looks. She is juxtaposing him against Titus, though perhaps accidentally. I wonder whether she's hoping to paint her progeny into something less frail than he. I wonder whether she is perpetuating tall tales to enhance her illusion of stability.

She continues, and were she aware she would notice that the nurse is not engaged but instead only saying "mmm-hmm," and looking over the grandmother's shoulder. She makes eyes at me as if to apologize, as if to say, "I feel sorry for this poor woman's grandbaby." I feel the tension and make eyes back toward the nurse as if to say, "At only one, that kid has some big britches to fill."

Having heard enough about the woman's future hall-of-fame, presidential, wonder-genius, I grab the pole to which Titus's IV and feeding tube are attached and walk back toward our room. "Bye, honey," she says to Titus and he waves, oblivious to the heat of her insensitivities. People and their words lack intentionality sometimes. It's the way we are.

My telephone rings, and though I do not recognize the number, I answer. It is a member of my church, a man I know to be good. We share brief salutations, passing platitudes and he begins to tell his story. "I'd like to share a bit of hope with you," he says.

"My son was helplessly sick too. We happened to be visiting family just down from Children's Hospital when his heart stopped beating. We rushed him to the emergency room, prayed for a miracle, and by God's providence the docs were able to jump-start him. We would find that he had a rare disease, a wasting disease maybe a lot like Titus. We prayed for another miracle and God answered. He brought us the right doctor, or-chestrated every move, ordained the whole thing to bring healing and, ultimately, greater glory. God will bring you an answer in good time."

He means all the hope in the world, but I feel gut-punched. I am not in a particularly strong position of faith these days. I've been praying for answers, for growth and healing, and so far, none of it has worked. And now I'm listening to this creeping gospel of prosperity. "God will answer if you are faithful," he says.

He's telling a story of belief, and I am truly grateful for his reaching out. But these words don't bolster me; they feel more like a dagger than a comfort. Haven't I been faithful? Haven't I done right? And if my child were to pass to the next life, what does that say about my goodness? Worse yet, what does that say about God's?

He tells me to "hang on, keep faith in God. He is Titus's healer."

I would like to tell him that in this moment I'm not a man of particularly large faith. I'd like to tell him that I stopped praying for Titus's healing a week ago, and I'd kill for a sign, for a miracle doctor, for something to confirm I'm not walking some lonely road of damnation. I'd like to tell him that his words feel volume-less, like a milk-toast cop-out, that they mute the sting of the present. If I could, I'd tell him these promises seem myopic, an outcome-determinative view of the goodness of God.

But I don't.

"Sure. Thanks for calling," I say instead. There is no comfort in the effluence of men's words, I think. There's no vindication in them, either.

Titus is not yet one and he knows no better life than the one he is living. He carries joy through it all, oblivious to vanity that surrounds him, that which connects strength, intelligence and prosperity to God. It's not been an easy year, but he is being made into something tough. And as I learn to hold my tongue, as I extend grace to the weakest of word wielders, I am also being made tough; perhaps a bit more tender too.

Sometimes providence guards us from pain. Other times, the providence is in the pain. Lord, that we would understand the nuance and offer our words accordingly.

PAIN AND HOLY GROUND

Christina Gibson

AM AN UNNERVINGLY PRESENT PERSON. I rarely think about the future. I'm too caught up in the now to worry about what has to be done tomorrow. For some reason, pregnancy launched me into a preparatory nightmare. I couldn't be too equipped. I not only read infant books and "how to keep your kid out of therapy" articles, but I also read books on raising teenagers—just in case my kid walked out of the womb with a driver's license. But in all my forward thinking, I never thought about having a kid who couldn't go to Chuck E. Cheese.

Ellia has an illness—the kind where no one really knows what's wrong. The kind of disorder that only fifteen other people in the world have and that affects no one else in the United States.

Ellia stopped walking one day when she was two. The doctors were convinced she was faking, and a nurse put her in a room and told us that we wouldn't be seen until she stood up and walked. With her kidneys on the brink of failure, she somehow recovered a couple weeks later and learned how to sit up, stand and walk again.

This fluke illness came back with a vengeance. After a third paralytic episode and several near-death moments, Ellia was diagnosed with an extremely rare, life-threatening genetic disorder. Her skeletal muscle structure can break down when she gets any random, unpredictable illness. She loses muscle function from the neck down and, often, she risks multi-system organ failure. The pain is unbearable. All the doctors can do is offer support care. There is no known cure or treatment, and prognosis is uncertain.

Because of her illness, Ellia isn't supposed to be around germs. She's not supposed to climb in the PlayPlace at McDonald's. She's not supposed to go to public school where parents (like me) give their kids Tylenol to hide the fever and send their kids to class. And she certainly can't go to Chuck E. Cheese. There's not enough hand sanitizer in the world to clean that place up. All of a sudden, the world is a loaded germ gun pointed at my kid.

Despite our best efforts, our old-souled five-year-old knows what's going on. She knows what ICU means. She has asked me to look her in the eye and tell her whether or not she'll live to be a mommy.

The question makes me simultaneously hot and cold. I know how to put a kid in time out. But I'm not prepared to navigate this. I don't know how to talk to her about death. I don't know how to walk her through social isolation and fear.

The past few years have been a mixture of the frightening known and the debilitating unknown. I might as well use my parenting books as toilet paper. It has sunk in that no amount of preparation can help traverse these waters.

I don't always feel completely unprepared. After three years, I've become adept at taking an often nightly temperature and checking for leg pain and outsmarting Ellia when she's afraid to tell me it hurts. I've become better at not crying when the IV goes in or when she first sits in her wheelchair. But I've never gotten used to the part where I pack the bags to take to the hospital.

It's an out-of-body experience, light-headedly packing clothes and toys, thinking of what we're walking into—the pain, her questions about why I can't make it stop. In some ways I've learned what to anticipate. I know the nurses and doctors who adore Ellia. I know Ellia will want to watch *Gnomeo and Juliet* thirty times in English and twice in Spanish. But my familiarity with the situation doesn't eclipse the unknowns. I don't know if we'll be there two days or two weeks. I don't know how her kidneys will respond or if her lungs will collapse and she'll be intubated. I don't know how long it will be until she eats or takes a bath or gets to go to the playroom.

When I'm still at home, putting toothbrushes into that stupid bag, I face my own deep fears. I feel so vulnerable when the dread and mystery meet in Ellia's illness. Both are frightening. It's frightening to know what kind of pain she's in. It's unsettling to think of her lethargy, her emotional distress and mental distance, and my own what-ifs.

I hate pain.

And if I've learned anything the past few years, it's this: there is no way we can fully prepare ourselves for pain. You can brace for impact, but you can't stop it from hurting. Preparing for pain is a waste of time. We're far better off embracing difficulty instead of padding against it through cynicism, escapism or control.

I'm afraid to face the pain because it authors a frightening question: Is God going to be enough? No matter how much this hurts? The question slinks around inside of me despite my efforts to avoid its searing gaze.

The question crawls under my skin, into my heart, moves through my mind. I hear it like a voice in the garden: *Did God really say . . . ?* It's a snaky question because it gets in where we can't reach. It climbs into places of our past, present and future, demanding that God justify his whereabouts at different points in our lives. It loosens the bolts of faith and certainty, and we're not always sure how to put our belief back together. But the question only does damage when we're afraid of it.

Maybe it's a fair question—a good one, even. What if Ellia can't eat or her lungs collapse? Is God going to be enough? If we can't look this question in the face, if we're too afraid that the act of thinking the question will pull the drain out of our belief, then our faith is no faith at all.

The question is frightening. But if we don't squarely face the question of God's ability to take care of us, we'll not only be incapable of embracing the pain, we won't be able to fully embrace God.

For the first year after Ellia's diagnosis, I refused to embrace the pain or any deep theological questions. I wanted to escape. I wanted to avoid fear and anxiety, even if it meant rejecting the journey. In refusing to embrace the difficulty, it became clear that I was forfeiting the potential to meet with God.

I've found that in those positions of flux, in the horrible disappointments, I usually have the greatest opportunity for a sacred encounter. It's in the places I'm least likely to choose that I often meet with God. I don't know if it's because I'm more malleable or if God has a soft spot for suffering. But I do know that when we're stuck or hurting and our gut instinct is to run out of there as fast as we can, we are probably close to holy ground. It is in the very midst of our pain, the places we hate and the seasons of life we dread, that God's voice is most clear.

There's nothing pleasant about the frightening unknown, and there's nothing great about deep loss and loneliness. Those things are just inevitable. The real gift comes in God's willingness to turn our biggest challenges into landmark spiritual encounters—the kind of life-changing ones like Jacob's wrestling match with the angel or Hagar's conversation with the God who sees.

Questions and pain often hold hands on their way to my soul. It's up to me whether or not I let them in. Ignoring their knock will not block the hurt or the anxiety. I've learned survival requires us to face the known and the unknown alike, and to look for the sacred. I don't want to embrace pain, but I do want to embrace God. I think I'm finally learning to listen—even as I head to the hospital instead of Chuck E. Cheese. I'm learning, as I pack our hospital bags, that God might be saying, "Take off your shoes. You're standing on holy ground."

WHEN I PURSUED JOY

Monica Sharman

TWO OF OUR LITTLE ONES slipped away, never knowing breath
in their lungs or air on their pores. The first time, I was
thirteen weeks along. Check-up appointments had gone well
so far. My uterus seemed to be growing just right. Nausea
and fatigue, signs of a good pregnancy, assured me that this
baby was healthy. At the next appointment, we would listen
for the heartbeat.

But I never heard it. That baby's heart quit beating long ago.
At thirteen weeks I suspected something was wrong. Anxious
heartbeats pulsed somewhere in my throat while the doctor set
up the ultrasound, calmly chatting with me as he prepped the
wand with gel. My nervousness grew as he moved the cold
probe on my still growing belly.

I watched the screen as he worked but didn't know how to
interpret the image. All I saw was a black space. Empty. Which
was exactly the right way to interpret that ultrasound image.

"There's no baby," he said.

The obstetrician called it a "missed miscarriage," in which the embryo dies but the mother doesn't know it. Her *body* doesn't even know it yet; the placenta keeps growing as if it still has a baby to nourish. "The baby probably died very early on and then disintegrated, but for some reason the body thinks you're still pregnant." I nodded while the doctor explained and didn't sob until I was out in the parking lot.

A month later, I got pregnant again. At six weeks, we lost that one too.

After tears, fears still lingering, I prayed for another baby, then thanked God when I did not have to wait long.

But I did not maintain my gratitude.

Twelve weeks into the most physically and emotionally difficult pregnancy I ever had, instead of thanking God for giving me (so quickly!) what I asked for, I whined about other things I wanted but didn't have. I grumbled and complained.

I saw that joy no longer resided in me, and I resolved not to whine anymore but instead to focus on God's blessings and the reasons I had to be joyful.

I started pursuing joy; I made a plan. During this pregnancy, my emotional make-up and personality began to change. Drastically. Before, I had been an extreme introvert—your typical "engineer type"—who was perfectly content working all by myself in a dark lab for hours. I enjoyed being alone, never craved female friendships, and when people invited me to a girls' night out or a couples' progressive dinner, I thought, *Why would I want to do that?*

Then something happened. I noticed my internal changes and started referring to myself as "the new me." For the first time, I wanted girlfriends. I wanted a "best friend" girlfriend, and I started looking hard for a relationship (or three or four) like that.

So I sought out the company of others. I arranged weekly lunches with my husband. I invited families to dinner. I started saying yes to the girls' nights out. Fellowship, companionship, love—these things brought joy. My plan seemed to be working.

I brainstormed other ways to pursue joy and discovered that serving others through selfless deeds was another way to lift me from dark places: I brought a meal to a busy family, sent an encouraging note and changed a diaper for a young mother.

Grinning, I clenched my teeth, flexed my biceps and plowed on with my plan for joy. In between the highs, though, were deep lows of despair. I had to fight so hard to be joyful—but when it came, it was only momentary. My plan had flaws. The first few months of that pregnancy were the hardest months I had endured in a long time. I never knew emotional pain could be that excruciating and was tired of crying.

What happened? I thought I found the answer. I thought I cured myself of emotional instability by (1) refusing to complain and dwelling on positive things, and (2) pursuing things—good things like fellowship and selfless service—that bring me joy. The result was a frantic ride of intermittent joy followed by darkness, misery and despair.

If my plan for joy was failing, then what was the real answer? Where was hope? How could I get out?

Tears, and tears again. Real heart pain. And in the midst of it, hard, true, unwavering words from my husband, the father of the child alive and growing in me:

"I think you've been seeking satisfaction outside the Lord."

I didn't want to hear that and flung sharp words at him. "Then how *do* you seek joy in the Lord?" I demanded.

In his characteristic, deep-seated calm, my husband answered, "You actually don't. You seek the Lord, and he grants you joy."

I got my answer.

"And on that day they offered great sacrifices and rejoiced because *God had given* them great joy" (Neh 12:43 NASB, emphasis mine).

I had been a persistent hound with the goal of hunting joy, running it down on my own. But the joy I thought I achieved was as empty and deceiving as a womb that miscarries but still grows, thinking a baby is inside. This kind of "joy" was like the black center of the ultrasound screen. Empty. I was trying to nourish a baby that I didn't realize was already dead. Manufactured joy always miscarries. There's no real life in it.

God's Word does command me to rejoice, and in hard circumstances I should choose to rejoice instead of complain or sulk or despair. But joy is no longer my pursuit, no longer my end goal.

During those months, I learned a hymn by Frederick Brook I had never heard before: "My Goal Is God Himself." The first two lines alone spoke to the truth that was beginning to take root in me: "My goal is God himself, not joy, nor peace / Nor even blessing, but himself, my God." It was nearly an exact echo of what my husband told me. My end goal should be not joy but God himself.

I still exult in good, sweet companionship. I still do acts of service and enjoy it. But I no longer aim my sights at joy. *I pursue God himself.* Then he grants me joy, growing it in me. And joy like this is real, and it is alive.

WRESTLING WITH GOD IN THE ART HOUSE THEATER

Karissa Knox Sorrell

I'M SITTING IN A STALL of the art house theater bathroom, sobbing. There are only two stalls in here, only one sink—standing room for two people, maybe. *Small as a tomb*, I think.

Entombed. That's where he is.

Someone enters the bathroom. *Damn*, I think. But I can't stop crying.

"Are you okay?" she asks.

"I—I just didn't know what this movie was about," I answer.

"What movie?" she asks.

"*Tree of Life*."

"Oh. Yeah," she says.

Now I'm going to have to tell her. "I lost a brother. It's just brought it all back."

"Oh! I'm so sorry! How old was your brother?"

"Seventeen," I choke out between sobs.

"How terrible! You know, the thing about those things is the people who get left behind suffer the most," she offers.

I'm used to this. Platitudes. People trying to find something, anything, to say that might help. A few people told my parents it was God's will that my brother died because he was going to grow up to be a drug addict or something worse.

I don't believe that. And I hate it when people try to play God and outreason Someone who defies reason.

But this girl, this stranger on the other side of the stall, keeps trying to reach out.

"Well, I don't know you, but I'll give you a hug if you want." She has come out of her stall and is washing her hands.

I don't want to face her. "Um, no, that's okay. I'll be all right. But thanks," I say.

"Okay, well—I love you, and I'm sorry." I hear the creak of the bathroom door.

All my friends told me I had to see this movie. I think they've forgotten about Will. It's okay. It's been twelve years now. Long enough for everyone, except those who loved him, to forget.

When I first converted from Protestantism to Eastern Orthodoxy, one of the things I loved was the rich tradition of saints. I loved looking at the beautiful icons covering the walls of our church. I loved finding out the exciting and inspiring stories behind these godly men and women. I loved filtering through all these stories to find a saint I could call my own. It took a while before I realized that in Orthodoxy, the tradition of saints is more than just old stories.

We believe that during liturgy, heaven and earth come together to worship God. All the saints and angels and people who have died raise their voices with us in praise, thanksgiving and intercession. We step out of *chronos* time and into *kairos* time, God's time, time outside of time, unbound by clocks and hours and years. In some unexplainable mystery, we join hands with that great cloud of witnesses in the act of worship.

Because of this mysterious *kairos* time, Orthodoxy gives great focus to remembering the dead. When an Orthodox Christian dies and has been prepared for burial, there is an all-night vigil in which family, friends and church members take turns singing and praying. (In fact, we also do such a vigil on Holy Friday, or Good Friday, for Jesus.) Forty days after the death, the church remembers the deceased with Memorial Prayers, and the family makes a memorial food called *kolyva*, which is brought to the church to share with the congregation. Memorial Prayers are also often prayed on anniversaries of deaths. When someone dies, a typical Orthodox saying is, "Memory eternal."

Memory eternal. That's so much better than *rest in peace* or *he's in a better place now* or *it was God's will for your brother to hit the windshield of a van.* Memory eternal. Your loved one has died. We remember him. We know that his spirit lives eternally with God.

It's not reasoning or empty attempts at comforting. It's just stating the truth.

The most beautiful hymn in the Orthodox Church is the Paschal Hymn. *Pascha* is our word for Easter, and it is the most important event of the church year. The Paschal Hymn says,

Christ is risen from the dead
Trampling down death by death

And upon those in the tombs
Bestowing life

When we sing this at *Pascha*, we hold our blazing candles high in the air. We shout it, announce it like we believe it, like we know it's true. We are so drunk on Christ's resurrection that we laugh ecstatically, then we cry a little, then we laugh again.

The time of year that I most want to see Will's face again is *Pascha*. It's when I sing those words: *and upon those in the tombs bestowing life*. I know, deep in my soul, that Will is not in that casket, not in that underground tomb. That's just his shell. I know he's alive. It doesn't make me miss him less or wish he hadn't been killed. But I can't sing those words, I can't be a part of that resurrection jubilee, without believing that somehow, somewhere, somewhen, my brother is alive.

I finally make it back to my seat in the theater. The tears don't stop, but they're under control now. I keep watching. Everything about this movie spells grief.

The camera shots: unusual, sideways, angled—that's how it is when someone dies. Everything is out of place, jumbled, uncomfortable, backwards. No truth is upright anymore.

Everything created: the burning fires of the sun, the depths of the ocean brimming with gorgeous creatures, the sky full of wings—all of that incredible creation collapses when part of it stops breathing.

The music: It could be the soundtrack to my childhood— the piano and organ, watching my mother's hands and feet moving across keys and pedals, listening to my father's tenor voice flowing all over the house. And then, it stopped. Dammed up. Silence.

I cringe when the older brother says, "Where were you? You let a boy die." It is me. I am the older sibling, always expected to do right. I am walking through that desert, searching for Will, searching for that perfect family that I lost.

I can forgive Will. I can forgive him for not wearing a helmet, even for getting on a motorcycle when he knew Mom and Dad didn't want him to.

But I can't forgive God. Twelve years, and I still can't quite forgive him. I can't forgive God for not answering my mother's prayer that day to keep her *son safe*. I can't forgive God for not intervening somehow. I can't pray without wondering if God really exists or if he can hear me or if he will say no. I can't think about Will without wondering, like the mother in the movie, *God, why?*

When the older brother in the movie wanders through the desert, I think about the passage in Genesis when Jacob wrestles with God:

> Then Jacob was left alone; and a man wrestled with him until the breaking of day. Now when He saw He did not prevail against him, He touched the socket of his hip; and the socket of Jacob's hip was dislocated as he wrestled with Him. Then He said, "Let Me go, for the day breaks." But he said, "I will not let You go unless You bless me." So He said to him, "What is your name?" He said, "Jacob." And he said, "Your name shall no longer be called Jacob, but Israel; for you have prevailed with God and with men." Then Jacob asked, saying, "Tell me Your name, I pray." (Gen 32:24-29 Orthodox Study Bible)

I am a lot like Jacob, just fightin' it out with God all night in the middle of the scary dark. Jacob doesn't even know it's God. What strikes me in this story is that God seemed to be close to losing! Part of me thinks it was good sportsmanship for God to level the playing field for the fight. But I also wonder if God allows himself to be weak sometimes. Or chooses to limit himself. Or he's not as cut-and-dry as we make him out to be—a multifaceted mystery.

Then Jacob doesn't let go. He demands a blessing, he demands to know his opponent. And God names not only himself but Jacob. Renames. Reshapes. Remolds. Jacob is now Israel, *One Who Wrestles with God*.

When I think of Will's death and other human suffering, this is the best I can do: bad things happen. Terrible things happen. Humans suffer. *God is with us.* He works for good in the midst of terrible circumstances. And on those days that I wrestle so hard with him that I am bruised and battered, like Jacob I cry out, "Tell me your name! Remind me of who you are!" In desperation, in my near faithlessness, I still cling to the small hope that he's real and he loves. *I will not let you go unless you bless me. Remold me into who you want me to be.*

"I love you, and I'm sorry," said the girl in the theater bathroom. I never saw her face and didn't even get a glimpse of her shoes. Maybe I should have come out of that stall and let her hug me. Maybe she was an angel in disguise sent to comfort me. Maybe she was God in disguise, come to find me. Come to name me. Come to bless me. And I turned away.

But I didn't forget it. I still think about those moments in that tomb of a bathroom. One night, I told a stranger my truth—and she told me she loved me. I will always remember.

A BROKEN LOVE STORY

Lindsey van Niekerk

T FELT LIKE THE WORST BREAKUP OF MY LIFE.
You know the one. The one that leaves you with more questions than answers. The one that makes you wonder what you did wrong. The one that takes the love in your heart and squeezes out every drop of blood and somehow you still love anyway. The one that makes you cry and wish you could walk away, but somehow the love you experienced was so real that you know in your heart of hearts that you could never really and truly walk away.

That is what happened to me and church.

My life began in a juxtaposition of sorts. Born white in a black world, American blood with Haitian air first breathed into my lungs, I grew up a third-culture kid, belonging neither to the country of my parents nor the country of my birth. As a missionary kid, I spent most of my days speaking more of the language of the native people than the one from which my heritage would dictate me speak.

And Jesus was real. Not just a Sunday school Jesus but real-life, gritty, in-the-midst-of-the-hard-circumstance Jesus. And I loved him and accepted him and longed to know him better and better from the time I was four years old. I believed him, his words, his heart. I knew beyond a shadow of a doubt that it was true and real and oh-so-right.

Life was not easy. We lived through frequent gunfire, bomb threats to the mission compound, early curfews, prejudice from skin color or nationality, homesickness, school cancellations for political instability, foreigner evacuations, transition from dictatorship to democracy. But in the journey, we learned how to praise, how to find the silver lining, how to laugh in every circumstance. My mom would inspire us with old praise choruses that we would morph into our own:

Praise him.
Praise him.
Praise him when the generator's broke.
Praise him with the truck is broken down.
Praise him.
Praise him.
Praise him when you're stuck at home in the dark.

And then there was church—a central part of our upbringing. Mom taught us Sunday school for years when we had no other English alternatives. We attended English missionary services. We had family devotions. We gathered in community as often as we could. I loved the fellowship, the family environment, the safety I felt there.

Armed with this courage and perspective that I would soon learn was beyond my years, I headed to Oklahoma to fulfill my desire for higher education. Being at a Christian university, the love fest continued in my relationship with Jesus and especially my longing to connect to the local church. I found the most amazing friendships that a girl could ask for, proving that college really is one of the most incredible times of life. We all attended the coolest church together on Friday nights and later on Sunday mornings too. The pastor was honest and real and relevant. The worship was open and transparent. The environment was ripe for growth. My roommate and I began to volunteer in the children's ministry, even sacrificing watching the big Christmas play event of the year so we could love on the rambunctious toddlers. I loved it all. Every. Single. Minute.

Attending a well-known evangelical university and a popular, up-and-coming church had its pitfalls. There was major upheaval of our campus pastor due to jealousies of his influence and pride of the administration that created a rift in our once relatively peaceful community. Simultaneously, my church's senior pastor confessed to a ten-month-long affair, exposing himself and his family to intense scrutiny. That same year, I graduated and moved back to my stateside home.

After months of paddling my way through the murky waters of lying, brokenness, sorrow and misunderstandings, I found my heart only more determined to find a way for this church dynamic to be pure. To discover the beauty that God intended in the body of Christ was a worthy aim in my book, and I strove to plumb the depths of all its glorious possibilities.

It took a while. I hit a few road blocks in my desire to serve and to connect, but after a few years, I finally found a church family that I loved and that was willing to use me even though

I was single, which I have since discovered is pretty progressive in this culture.

I was a youth leader, and we had an amazing team who worked together. It was hard work but very rewarding, and our team worked hard and played hard together, which was simply the best.

The years went by, and living and working in a small town as a single woman became increasingly alienating, but not when I was at church. There I was the cool girl who did not *need* a guy to be whole; my talks were relevant to the teen girls and their own struggles with appearance, sexuality and loneliness.

Finally, in what was a whirlwind six months, God sent my future husband from South Africa to our little town to work with the children of my church. We fell in love, got married and began our married life in the thick of full-time ministry with kids and teens surrounding us almost daily.

The first year was hard. And that sentence is an understatement. Striving for balance and finding none quickly, I plumbed the depths of myself, struggling to understand this new role as wife and pastor simultaneously. After twelve months of internal and external wrestling, along with depression, I received wise advice from my husband's mentor. "You are not called to be just *anyone's* wife, you are called to be *Arno's* wife." It pulled my perfectionist soul back to reality. And the next year seemed to move forward with ease until we felt the Lord calling us to Africa. But the leaving felt more like tearing. Bumps and bruises along the journey became mountains of misunderstandings. Release to go was hard-won, and saying goodbye for this little missionary girl all grown up was just as hard, and maybe more so, than the very first time I ever did so.

The South African adventure became the best and the worst time of my life. I learned my limits and my boundaries. I found new capacities for success and human connection that surprised and delighted me. I discovered the depths of pain a human soul could experience and somehow still find a road to redemption.

It is funny to me that those three years could be summarized in four short sentences because that season was anything but short, felt anything but redemptive, and found me anything but joyful for months on end.

With passion and fervor, my love and I tackled and pounced on every task and obstacle given to us in that first year. We also decided that it was time to begin to expand our little family after two and a half years of marriage. Simultaneously, my health began to dip and decline. I chalked that up to the transition and my body's adjustment to the African climate. Although having grown up in Haiti relatively healthy for most of my upbringing, I wondered at my body's inability to stabilize.

In the second year, the pace at which we engaged in ministry life there had to be adjusted. We began to find our rhythm in some ways and grappled in others as the honeymoon period faded and real life set into place. The chronic nature of the health issues continued to plague me, and after a year and a half of trying for a baby to no avail, my spirit waned.

Why had God forsaken me in this foreign land? Why had he led me so far from home, homesick for my family, to deny me my heart's desire, to ask me to bear this physical burden, to place ministry challenges in the form of faces and names that would not budge, to abandon me? Why did he hate me? My heart cried over and over again, desperate for answers that did not come.

Months went by with bipolar type feelings—happy/sad, content/overwhelmed, peaceful/miserable on any given day, at any given moment.

On January 12, 2010, when the 7.0 earthquake ravaged the island of my birth, the bottom of my already-tumultuous world fell apart. In an agonizing seventeen-hour wait to know if my parents were dead or alive, my soul died a thousand deaths. In the months to follow, the challenges became mountain ranges to overcome, and in my warzone of a heart, life took on a fog-laden view.

Loving people had been my life's goal, and now I felt incapable of giving or loving the way I knew they deserved. Drowning in my own anxieties and sorrow, my too-late cries for help were met with mixed signals and confusing expectations. Support and the bottom line were never far from each other, and while some part of me understood, the level of brokenness to which I had arrived left me barely keeping my head above water like a victim of my own personal *Titanic*. Life rafts were not readily available, and many days I longed to surrender to the icy waters that threatened to overtake me.

After a lifetime of full-time ministry, as a child, a single woman and a married couple, my husband and I made the impossible decision to step down from full-time ministry and head back to America for an indefinite season of rest and recuperation.

More than two years later, after some counseling and time "away from the front lines," I have learned a lot—mostly that I still have so much more to learn.

My love, church, and I are slowly finding our way back to each other. We found a local place where we could just sit and *be* for a while, and while my attendance has been spotty at best—

mostly due to, but not limited to, physical health issues—I realize that I am not a "date around" kind of girl, nor am I a girl who can "keep it casual" in a relationship. I am not sure how to be a regular part of a church congregation without being involved, yet I do not know how to "be involved" without feeling like I am surrendering myself to the wills of the powers that be in a way that may cause me further detriment.

And there is the rub.

How do I move forward? How do I go back to the love that I know to be true yet has caused me pain?

I will tell you now. This story does not end with all the answers or complete resolution.

I suffer daily from chronic pain.

Our road into parenthood has been anything but easy.

Attending church grips my heart in panic almost every time.

And yet.

This journey has caused me to discover myself in ways that are only possible in a pilgrimage led by the Father. While many dreams are still out of reach, and I often wonder at how my life looks nothing like the plan in my head, I am more real and true and open to the person that the Creator made me to be. I have more grace for not only my story but also the stories of those around me. I have found a love in my Savior that rivals the fairytale version I once knew.

I am a book filled with torn, well-worn pages that sing of a life ravished by grace alone.

This is my love story.

METAMORPHOSIS

Joy Bennett

SOMETIMES I LOOK AT PHOTOS OF MYSELF from earlier years—high school, college and even my wedding—and my heart aches for that younger version of me. I see the innocence and joy on my face, the unbridled optimism, the enthusiasm for change and making things better, and I cringe, knowing the pessimism, grief, cynicism and despair that lie ahead.

Just seventeen months after my husband and I were married, our first baby was born, and we were plunged into life as parents of a medically fragile child. We felt our way through every moment of those first months and years, wavering between hoping for miracles and bracing for tragedy as our baby girl wobbled atop the knife's edge of death. We discovered strength we didn't know we had inside as we fought for her life. I learned skills I never dreamed I'd need, like inserting a feeding tube through my infant's nose and down into her stomach. I had been the child who hid from the nurse when she came to give shots, but I became the mother who gave them to her child.

As our baby grew, I learned to trust my instincts with her. I developed the ability to detect subtle changes in her and predict what the doctors would find. I remember one day before a cardiology checkup, I told my husband that I thought they were going to find some problems.

"I think she's going to need a stent, honey. Something isn't quite right."

He dismissed my prediction. Unlike me, he preferred to face bad news when it arrived, not ahead of time.

Before the tests, the nurses asked me how I thought our daughter was doing. I told them of my concerns, though I couldn't quite put my finger on any one specific thing. Sure enough, the echocardiogram of our daughter's heart showed narrowing that would require a procedure to open and stent it.

This same instinct took honing for each additional child. I overreacted with each of them at the beginning. I was on high alert because of the experiences I'd had with our first child, but I didn't need to be. Gradually, I learned how different each of our children are, and I learned (and am still learning) how to read them. Our youngest also has a chronic condition, but very little of what I learned about reading our oldest applied to him.

I have always believed in a God who loves us and who made a way for us to be in right relationship with him. What that means for the tragedies of life has changed through our years with our children. Before they were born, I had a naive, Pollyanna trust that God was in control of all circumstances and that faith in him could carry us through any pain and any tragedy. At first, it did carry me through.

But as the years of fighting death back from our daughter's bedside wore on and as her condition worsened, I began to doubt that God was good.

A friend put it this way. "I know that God *can* answer my prayers and change situations and do good things. But I don't think that he *will*."

I think it was a defense against the loss I knew was coming. I knew that our daughter would die before we did. I hated being blindsided by bad news, so I braced myself for the worst. But you can only do that for so long before you start to see God that way too, as someone with the power to change things but without the will to do so. I began to wonder if God got some sort of sadistic pleasure from seeing how long creatures who depended on him would trust and love him. How much could he put them through and still maintain their devotion? Were we all a giant Job-esque experiment?

Those doubts of the goodness of God led me down a dark path of questions. I realized that my Pollyanna faith couldn't stand under the relentless pressure we were under. Something was inherently flawed in it, and no matter what I did to cobble a repair, it continued to crumble.

This new skeptical version of me found herself trapped in a miserable situation. In public, I was the wife of a leader in our church. We were examples of faithful servants of God, trusting him in the face of incredible trial. We led the singing on Sunday mornings, me at the piano with a microphone in my face, proclaiming God's love to everyone. But in private, I was questioning everything, and eventually I started over. I asked myself that first question, *Does God exist?*

I couldn't very well tell anyone of my questions, so I buried them, wrestling in my soul, pouring out tearful prayers in the shower as I begged God to find me if he really existed. But the dissonance nearly choked me. I hated myself for my fakery.

In the midst of that crisis of faith, we awoke one morning to find our daughter unresponsive. We became bereaved parents as suddenly and as painfully as we had become special needs parents just eight and a half years earlier, in the hospital's emergency department at the words of a doctor bearing bad news.

Six months later, we closed the doors on a church we'd poured five years of ourselves into.

In spite of that double loss, I didn't get help. I'd been indoctrinated into the idea that secular psychology couldn't be trusted and that real Christians could triumph with the right attitude. But this so-called biblical alternative proved impotent in the face of this perfect storm.

Two years after my daughter died, my son slid a drawing under my bedroom door. He had drawn a picture of me yelling at his brother and wrote a plea for me to stop. I stared at that crude representation of who I had become and my body shook with desperate sobs. The woman who had held things together for so many years was gone. My grief had disintegrated into an angry and volatile depression, and my family lived terrified of the next outburst.

I couldn't live like that anymore. I saw a doctor and after some tests to make sure something else wasn't going on, I began taking antidepressants. I began writing more honestly about my doubts and questions, about how bad things were, and about how I was trying to put the pieces back together. Like a cast stabilizes a broken bone while it heals, the medications gave me enough stability to do the hard work of reconstructing my life and my faith. Being open and honest freed me from the chokehold of pretense and hypocrisy.

It has taken years, and I may never be able to go off antidepressants. But today, my faith in God, while nothing like it was before, is more flexible, more able to bend with the pain of life, not break. Today my children don't walk on eggshells around me. Today I can share my story without bitterness. Today I'm less afraid of the backlash from those who are comfortable behind the pretense.

Sometimes I think about what lies ahead of me. I wonder how many more versions of me are yet to emerge. I shudder at the inevitable pain that seems to always accompany this metamorphosis.

But then I step back and realize that wisdom and maturity are a mixture of all of these. My innocence needed to be strengthened by experience, my joy has been deepened by grief, my optimism and enthusiasm are grounded in reality. I am more discerning today. I appreciate more deeply and broadly today. I have more realistic expectations, especially of my fellow human beings who cannot help but disappoint in the same ways that I too disappoint. I have more grace to give, especially to those who make mistakes and to those who find themselves broken by life. Just as important, I have more grace for myself: for the persistence of my weaknesses and flaws, for the extended time I need to develop my strengths and gifts and for all the as-yet-undiscovered iterations of myself.

BREATHING ROOM

Tanya Marlow

SAT IN MY LIVING ROOM surrounded by friends who were discussing the latest book for our book club. Their words buzzed around me while I battled the emotion rising in my chest.

My stomach tightened and I resolved again: *I will do it. I will talk about this book without crying and they will not see the desperation in me.*

The book seemed innocuous enough and distant enough from my experience. *Room,* by Emma Donoghue, is about a woman who is abducted, imprisoned in a twelve-foot-square air-conditioned shed and raped daily by her captor. She becomes pregnant and, despite the nature of his conception, loves her baby deeply and spends her days finding ways of keeping him entertained and educated. The novel is about how they try to escape from their captor by pretending the boy has died.

Reading the back cover, it seemed sufficiently removed from my experience that it wouldn't touch any nerves. After all, I had never been kidnapped or raped.

But as I read it, I found it unlocked a deep pain.

Prior to giving birth, I was only well enough to work part time and could walk just a short distance before becoming exhausted. I had myalgic encephalomyelitis, a poorly understood auto-immune neurological condition. Physical exertion, however slight, worsens symptoms and can cause a severe relapse.

My physicians assured me that there was no reason why going through labor should present any risk to me having an ME relapse. They were wrong.

The day after I gave birth I awoke in agonizing pain and found myself in a terrifying new world of disability. I was unable to stand up or walk at all. I had to be helped to the bathroom. I was breathless and experienced tachycardia every time I sat up.

Childbirth had crashed and battered my body, splintering and shipwrecking my health. One month on, I still couldn't walk more than a few paces and was virtually bedbound. I had to be carried upstairs because I couldn't manage by myself, and we had to permanently change our bedroom to the one nearest the bathroom. I couldn't maintain a conversation for longer than thirty minutes before reaching a state of complete exhaustion.

I couldn't walk, I couldn't talk; I was as helpless as the baby I was supposed to be looking after. Spluttering, flailing, terrified, I was treading water and concentrating on keeping alive. All I could do was eat, nurse my baby and lie in bed. My husband had to do the rest.

For the first year of my son's life, I lived almost entirely in one room where I looked after him. Even now, two years on, I can only leave the house for a glorious, magical hour or two, once a week, in a wheelchair. On a bad month, I can barely go downstairs.

It is probably for this reason that I felt a bond with this fictional mother; we had so much in common. The boy who narrated the story loved his mother and loved his life despite his captivity. He didn't know any different. In a place that felt like failure, these characters offered me hope.

The mother in the book invented games for her son to play to keep physically and mentally active—hopping over furniture, imaginative play, memory games reciting what they'd just heard on the television. It sounded almost idyllic, the close bond between mother and child. Each day was an adventure played out in the small room. Even the shouting for help was disguised as a game.

I found myself taking notes, challenging myself to come up with better games for my baby. We played the "keep the baby entertained on the bed for as long as possible so he doesn't crawl off" game. We sang songs, and my hands told the story along with my voice. I pushed shapes through holes or hid objects under the covers while he stared, fascinated. I recited nonsense rhymes until his giggles erupted into the air with pure, molten pleasure.

And we read. We disappeared into books—worlds where bears popped out from cupboards, porridge was everlasting and flooded the house, pigs ran away from wolves, puppets moved independently and became alive. We delighted in the ridiculous, the incredible. We inhabited the imaginary. We read for three hours or more each day. I relaxed into every sing-song phrase, the same stories, the repetitive rhymes, not begrudging a single word because how many other activities can you do with an under-one-year-old to keep them entertained for hours in a day?

Flotsam and jetsam could be found, and I grabbed what I could. The bed strewn with toys and books and cushions became a life-saving raft. I was Robinson Crusoe, finding a new land and making our home there.

And there were days when I felt like the young boy in the book: this was my world, and we were safe. Mother and child, we had our universe and we had fun together, and it was enough—the fun and the love and the milk I gave him, and I could do this.

Then there were the days when I felt like the mother in the book, and the world was just unbearably small, the walls too beige, my reading voice too feeble and solitary. The minutes lengthened and yawned before me; I looked into the future and all I could see was a great unending chasm of time. The boy grew bigger, but time seemed to have paused, each day like the one before.

The initial chapters of *Room* described the characters' life together, and I found myself comforted by the variety of their routine and the largeness of their inner world, despite their physical limitations. *At least I can get out once a week or so,* I thought to myself. *At least I have my husband.*

The following chapters were all about whether they were going to escape and whether or not they would die. I sobbed through all one hundred remaining pages, feeling with her the intense longing to escape and the desire, above all, to protect her precious son.

I too was feeling the longing to escape but also the desire to protect my boy and keep him close to me. I loved and hated my baby's freedom. I loved that my husband and later a string of nannies took him on various outings, to see life properly in Technicolor. I hated that he needed a world outside of me, that I wasn't enough.

I found myself fiercely decrying nurseries and play groups as unnecessary and for the mothers' benefit rather than the children. I was asked repeatedly by anxious, hovering, medical and social services professionals, "He is getting out, isn't he? We don't want him to be a prisoner in his own house," and I was hot with indignation. Some people abandon their children at the age of six weeks to be looked after in a crowded room by strangers in a nursery, and yet I am the one you are criticizing? I, who have loved him and can provide everything he needs? We are fine. Just look at our life; we have so much fun. Just like the book, this child loves it, he's happy with his mother, he wants for nothing.

I was defensive and defiant and making it work with limited resources. I had only sticks and string, but we were afloat.

Just reading *Room* had been a cathartic experience for me, and I sobbed out the devotion and sorrow for my boy throughout the pages of the book. I told myself I got it out of my system and I could now enjoy the book club without getting overly emotional. I could be the friendly, chatty, fascinating person that my friends were familiar with.

I would not be the invalid. I would not waste this rare social opportunity by making people feel like I was miserable the whole time. I would not cry.

One by one, my friends talked about the opening chapters of the book—those chapters that had breathed life into me, in which I had learned that life even in a small room could be full of adventure and variety and fun.

"Those opening chapters were so boring and repetitive," they said.

"I felt so claustrophobic reading them. It was just the same thing every day."

I had not prepared myself for this. I had thought that I was in the same mothering world that they were, doing what regular mothers do. I discovered that my most interesting and entertaining morning would be their idea of rainy-day hell.

I suddenly felt like a tired balloon. At that moment, I saw the reality of my life and its smallness and its claustrophobia: the beige walls, the constant noise of cars passing, the watching of the clock, the lonely tears, the brave smiles, the stifling silence. I saw the isolation and the endlessness.

"And what did you think of the book, Tanya?" they asked.

I tried.

I spoke; the word died in my throat. I opened my mouth again, but the emotion pressed onto my chest, squeezing my breath, spewing forth a calescent stream of tears. The sobs came out deep from my stomach like animal, visceral groaning.

The others were silent, surprised, unsure.

Several minutes passed while I cried wordlessly, helplessly. Eventually I managed to speak: "It was just *too* close. Those opening chapters that you found so repugnant? Those are my life."

Sometimes it takes a stranger, even a fictional character, to show us our life. It helps us connect. I had squashed it all down with months of "it's okay, really," and in that moment I saw how un-okay it was. I wept, vomiting tears and months of silence, because it was finally okay not to be okay.

And so I tell my story, my moment of weakness and emptiness where I could do nothing but pour myself out in tears, because someone's story helped me to find those tears.

Sometimes even the tears are a gift.

Part Three

HOPE AND HEALING

TIE TO THE DEEP

Tara Pohlkotte

SOME OF MY EARLIEST MEMORIES were formed with my back pressed against the hard pew, watching my daddy's legs pace the podium behind his pulpit. I was transfixed by the rise and fall of his voice as I watched the worn, gold-plated pages in his hands catch the sun from the tiny stained-glass window while he spoke words that were written by men centuries before. And I believed undoubtedly in these words—in these stories of kings and creation, anointment and redemption, and betrayal, adultery and murder. Stories that brought you to the height of divine power and into the depths of the fallen race. It never occurred to me to question what I was taught. My parents' faith blindly became my own.

Then, on a February morning, the frozen earth was broken open to receive my biggest champion. The starkness of the fresh soil against the snow mirrored the way my heart felt trying to accept the world without my grandfather in it. The north wind blew hard around us, and my nine-year-old hand reached for my brother's as the taps played. It was then, when we scarred the belly of the earth, returning my papa to its womb, that I began to understand that the God I had been taught about would not satisfy. This version of living would not be enough for me. There had to be more than felt Bible figures. My Savior would not stand before me smiling in pure white robes—not when every time I closed my eyes, all I saw was fresh dirt hitting mahogany. My world would no longer accept him as a fairy-tale knight in shining armor. He would come to me tearing his gown, with a tear-stained face and hands black from going into the grave to redeem.

Over time, I grew to understand that my concept of the Christian faith would need to be rebuilt. I stopped being disappointed he did not come to me on Sunday mornings. I stopped looking for him within the confines of church walls. Rarely do I see his face bathed in sunlight. Instead, he finds me under the shade of pines. He comes to me when I'm not afraid of the deep places within myself, when I actively look for the core of my fellow humans. He comes to me dressed as neighbors, as tattooed friends who don't believe. He comes as a soul sister, our twin beds pressed up next to each other as we talk deep into the night. He comes to me as the oppressed, as the blessed. He comes to me most deeply as two children reaching for my hand.

Yes, more than anything, motherhood has furthered this exploration and expansion of what I know to be true about our deep faith places. I have learned that strength does not mean isolation. That true strength lies in giving of our heart, of putting our soul outside ourselves and watching it walk its imperfect way into the world. The very act of giving birth draws me further in. There is nothing more feral, more raw, than groaning with the pain of bringing forth humanity, nothing more divine than seeing the face of God pressed up to your breast—all of those seeming impurities of body and divinity joining together to bring forth a soul. We are born bathed in blood, our bodies intertwined with another's, emerging from this sacred place where we were knit together in the dark wrapped only with the pulsing rhythm of heart meeting vein. We grow without understanding our life is dependent on another. We nourish without a complete understanding of how our body sustains. Mother and child unknown to one another but fused together.

Our very navels mark our bodies with this symbol of interdependence. Permanently pressed into our skin is the sign that we belong to one another. That we could not grow without clinging to another for substance. That while we were still being woven together, we were being brought into the very belly of humanity. Life can only come from the dark shadows formed in mystery and grace. We were made to bend, to carry and to hold one another. We were not made alone nor of our own strength. We were made to feed and to eat, to nourish and to grow, to sustain and to receive. And we keep repeating this cycle. We are folded back into each other, into our making. Through this, we are able to tap into the majesty of our spiritual selves and feel the pain of being but dust in our depravity. When is it that we begin to fear the sight of blood, that which was our one comfort? To fear death—the returning into the very dark in which we were created? We, in our most broken and most holy of ways, are all one. Intertwined.

This exploration of our interconnection I found in motherhood led me to understand that, while I had since walked away from the organized church of my youth, I had not done away with communion. My chapel has become as expansive as the sky.

Every story I shared with another soul—every night spent in a smoky basement bar talking about the fullness of life, of dreams—brought me back shoulder to shoulder with the congregation of humanity. Reading words penned by hands I had never met provided me a wafer, the sacrament of their life told out. Every tear we shed pools and forms the cup of life. Our prayers need no words; we pray through showing up. We bare witness to one another in the dark, lying on the floor, bodies keeping vigil until the sun has returned. We help one another write our own scriptures—the passages that tell our lives, our struggles, dreams and celebrations. Tell me the gospel of where you've cut your heart open, the jagged scar that has healed and given hills to your valleys. Let us expose our scarred chests in the moonlight, explain the history of how we got each tattered one. Through our telling, let us see the beauty of looking at its origin, what it means to us now, and have honor for how it came to be. In that moonlight, it will not only be our skin that shines but also our souls—raw and gloriously exposed.

For now, far from the confines of a faith shaped by my daddy's pews, I know that to be born of the divinity of the stars woven together by dust leaves heartbreak. It leaves empty space between our marrow and our bone. I also know that the beauty of this world comes from bearing witness to it—to call it to ourselves, not to save or to overcome, but to love. And honest love, as ever I have found it, has left me weak and broken. So sit awhile, rest back into the womb that holds us all, draw life through our shared cord of love and strength. Let us feel our tie to the deep.

TEENAGE HERETIC

Amy Peterson

AT THE TOP OF THE GRAY WOOD TOWER, I lean, straight back, over the edge and down. The soles of my feet touch the corner of the platform, and I'm suspended over nothing, my body perpendicular to the wall. Left hand clasping the rope by my belly button, my right hand circles it loosely at the small of my back. I'm shaking the first time, but I step, then jump. I fly.

The next time, I push out and spin in a circle in the air before my feet hit the wall again. I tap dance down the side of the tower. The third time I rappel backwards, face first. I'm the only camper allowed to try that, and this fact makes me strong, confident in my nine-year-old body.

As a child, I lived equally in two worlds. The "real" world, where I biked, swam and rode horseback, and the equally real interior world where my bike took flight, I swam with dolphins, and the horses I rode were the Black Stallion and Misty of Chincoteague. I was as happy clambering up trees as I was sitting in my reading nook devouring a stack of books. I was as comfortable in my body as I was in my mind.

Days are long and curiosity abounds in childhood. Bored one afternoon, my best friend Olivia and I rolled on her parents' waterbed and played Truth or Dare. Soon we were mostly naked. I don't know why, exactly. We were innocent of and uninterested in sex, but curious about our bodies. How did they work? Were they the same?

I suppose it was also the allure of the forbidden: nakedness. We weren't even allowed to talk about body parts or body functions, and if we did, it was in quiet, buttoned-up voices, using words like *chest* and *bottom* and *passing gas*, never the words other kids used: *boobs* or *butt* or *fart*. All in all, it was better to pretend these things didn't exist.

Olivia's mom came in. She glanced at the bed, and then her eyes hit the floor, horror evident on her face. "What are you girls doing? Are you pretending to be married?"

Pretending to be married? Sometimes mothers were crazy, I thought. What does being married have to do with being naked in a bedroom? The look on her face made me feel shame, shame that I pushed deep down even as I imagined what she must have thought we were doing.

"I'm going to have to call your mother," she said.

From Olivia's well-intentioned mother I learned that curiosity about my body was something to be ashamed of, and curiosity about what married people did in bed, naked, was even worse. None of us ever spoke about it again. For the first time, I felt unsure about my body and whether it was essentially good or evil, capable or shameful.

As I got older, my body became less trustworthy.

We moved to a new city when I was eleven, and I joined a summer softball team. My teammates, who had grown up together, seemed to my insecure eyes to be very athletic miniature southern belles. I stood alone in left field and prayed the ball would never come to me and that the summer would end. My body was a foreign object, and I was too uncoordinated to connect the bat to the ball, and too afraid of failing to really try.

We didn't speak much of the body in my family. When I wanted to start shaving my legs, I crept into my mother's bathroom, took the razor and did it. In my mind, to discuss it would be tantamount to admitting that my body was changing, that I was becoming a sexual being—and that was shameful. It must be shameful, I thought, because no one ever spoke about it.

The early church battled the Gnostic heresy that the material world is inherently evil, something to be escaped rather than embraced. In adolescence, I became a gnostic Christian, distancing myself from my awkward body and cultivating instead a rich inner landscape. I didn't play sports, I never danced and I never kissed. I journaled and I joined the theater club where I could pretend to be in someone else's body.

It was a heresy that fit my personality. I was naturally drawn to the life of the mind, arguing like a lawyer at thirteen and losing myself in the other worlds of novels. In high school I became the president of the student council and the editor of the yearbook. I planned the dances, but usually spent them outside talking with my history teacher. I laid out the pictures on the pages, but I refused to get dressed up and have fancy senior portraits of my own made—a waste of money, I said, when we still have the poor with us; an image-obsessed vanity.

The church didn't exactly help me combat the gnostic heresy growing in my heart. If anything, the youth group's teaching about "True Love Waits" cemented my suspicion that my body was not to be trusted. My body was dangerous and likely to cause boys to "stumble." (Their bodies, on the other hand, were powder kegs, uncontrollable at the spark of my sleeveless shirt or too-short shorts.) Our bodies were best covered up and ignored because that was the only chance we had of keeping them pure "temples" of the Holy Spirit.

The church's party line encouraged my gnosticism, but it was through friendships at church that the wholeness of my childhood was returned to me. Maybe we didn't talk about our bodies at home—pretending that bums and breasts didn't exist—but my friends talked about their bodies, their breasts small and large, their bikini lines, their (gasp!) sexual desires. Elinor, a single woman ten years older than us, led our church small group. She seemed to understand that we were sheltered and fearful and distanced from the beauty of our bodies. Some of the church girls may have needed modesty talks and True Love Waits, but not us.

"Carpe Diem," she wrote in the front of our Bibles at graduation. "Go kiss a boy for the pleasure of it," she whispered in our ears.

A week later when Elinor took us to Gulf Shores for a graduation celebration, I wore a two-piece swimsuit for the first time. It was the eve of my eighteenth birthday, and we lounged in our condo, all limbs akimbo, damp hair and salty sunburned skin.

"Surprise!" Elinor came in the door bearing a birthday cake and a bottle of peach sparkling wine. My friends celebrated me, cutting and sharing the cake, pouring and passing the wine.

Later, under a big red moon, Mollie and I sat on the balcony, strumming chords and scratching lyrics on paper, experimenting with melodies.

Beth appeared, and someone said skinny dipping. Yes, I thought. Communion, song, baptism. God is here.

At the edge of the sandy gray beach, I slipped out of my clothes faster than anyone; they laughed at the flash of white butt as I ran into the water. Mollie followed and then Beth.

I dove deep, swam long, holding my breath; then broke the surface, delighting in the cool water touching my skin, and floating on my back, looking at the stars. My body felt capable and beautiful, as perfect a part of creation as this ocean, those stars, that big red moon.

Sometime later, chilled, we swam back. My clothes, and Mollie's, had disappeared, so we apportioned Beth's clothes and towel among us, giggling breathlessly up the beach to our condo as we ran fearlessly in toward the light.

LETTERS OF INTENTION

Sarah Bessey

WENT FOR A WALK in the fading of the day. I only have grace for one day, and today was nearly done. I layered our littlest girl all up, tucking her riotous curls into a little blue beret. The older two stayed at home with their dad. I needed a break, and in these busy days, one toddler feels like a rest. Even if it's just for an hour of evening sky gazing, this is me making space for joy.

It's truly autumn now, and I was breathing deep of freedom, of cool evenings, of wooly cardigans and darkness falling before the supper dishes are cleared. I pushed our consignment-shop stroller to the mailbox first.

There was a letter waiting there for me from my friend. I love to write letters, and I love to receive letters. In this age of texting and email, if there is one delight, it's spotting a real envelope in the slot with my name in cursive homely pen instead of the ironic typography of adverts or the businesslike serif of bill payments. Letters take a bit of time and intention to write; letters are more purposeful.

I'd been writing my first book, and now that it is finished, my friend knew I would be feeling a bit raw and exposed. She also knows that I am afraid: afraid of my calling, afraid of my own voice, afraid of stepping out onto the water. I am still undoing an old approval addiction. But years ago, when I fell in love with Jesus and his ways, I lost my barricades of apologetics, bravado, certainty and explanations. People pleasing leaves me heartsick.

Joy and calling, goodness and purpose arrived hand in hand with social justice and weakness, my awareness of suffering and newfound vulnerability. Part of me would like to ignore mothers in Newtown and Palestine; I'd like to forget about systemic injustice, hungry babies, sex trafficking, poverty and loneliness. It's uncomfortable to care. Every small bit I do feels inadequate. Sometimes I'd like to numb the cold dark creeping. But instead, I found my calling right in the midst of the vulnerability, and so I am writing and mothering and working and loving with ordinary bravery. I carried her letter with me to the field. Evelynn and I went up the hill and down the hill into the valley beside the Mennonite cemetery. Once we were safely away from the roads, I unbuckled the baby and set her free to wander. She promptly clawed into the dirt, scrabbling out small stones to present as jeweled offerings with great joy. She piled up dead leaves in the stroller's undercarriage.

She hollered with delight, nose running, mittens discarded, the light magnetized around her, mud under her fingernails. She was so incredibly happy. I crouched on my haunches, just to see her round face a bit better, and I filled my fleece pockets with her rocks and dirt and frozen, shriveled rose hips. Her cheeks were glowing rubies, and she was hard at play. By the last of the light, I read my friend's short letter, and she said good things to me, words of life and love. She wrote, "Don't forget that you're happier out here beyond the white picket fences . . . and when you are weak, He remains strong."

When the sun fell below the horizon, the light blazed out behind the pine trees. *This is it,* I thought as I stood up, back straight. This is my favorite sight: the inky blackness of pine trees, black lace relief burned out against the western sky as the last guardian of this date on the calendar cedes. It never lasts long, but it comes every day. Evelynn was still playing delight, and I stood, in the bright, cold silence, and the fading light fell on me, tired and glorious and spent. I felt wildly, inexplicably happy, I could see my breath. How is it that in this raw season, when I feel like my whole heart is thumping exposed, I have never been happier?

It's true. I've never been so spent yet so joyful. I've never been more convinced of my calling and yet scared to walk it out. I've never been more attuned to the suffering and yet quick to everyday joy. I've never been so easily wounded, and yet I love being armorless. I feel defenseless yet disinclined to pick up the sword.

I can't explain it, but I stood in the middle of the field that night with my arms open wide, the echoes of *Who do you think you are?* running away like mice while my littlest one filled her fingers with earth. *I'm her mama,* I thought, *I'm me, always. I'm yours, Jesus, always,* and I turned and surveyed my life like the gift it is, open to all that came my way for a little while anyway.

When it was time to go, I put Evelynn back into her stroller. She proceeded to scream the entire way back up the hill. Once she had tasted freedom, she could not go back to her tame little stroller. She fought the restraints, and I wondered if she would be so indignant if she hadn't been so happy being free. I wouldn't take her out—this isn't my first parenting rodeo—but once she calmed down, I put some of her rocks onto her little stroller tray to play with while we walked back down to our neighborhood. Maybe I could create a ministry of handwritten letters and twilight walks.

Isn't that the way of things these days—approach a leader to first ask for permission to be a minister, be properly trained, create a page on the website, pick a dynamic name for it? Maybe I could write a strategic plan and procure a marketing budget. Maybe I could organize and recruit a team, make sure that there is a policy and procedure for doing it right. We could prescribe walks to take that will best nourish the soul, and we will create a *revolution* of twilight letter writing and reading.

We could reach so many.

Or perhaps I will simply head home, fully alive, and in a few days write my friend back and work to remember that the bravest thing we can do is keep showing up in our real, right-now lives with love and joy and intention.

Perhaps this is the way of it, the way to leave behind the idea that loving well is an official thing, best left to others, or by simply writing a check to the professionals or partaking of a program. Perhaps I will be a person, see the person, make space for God, for truth, for beauty, for passion, for letters, for intentional love in my everyday, walking around world.

I'll write the words of Mother Teresa on a letter to my friend, put a stamp on it and mail it to California. In a week or two, she'll open her mailbox and walk along in the twilight, reading my letter and it will say, "If you can't feed thousands, feed one. Do small acts with great love."

Perhaps I will be a person instead of a ministry; perhaps I will remember we are people, not ministry opportunities to be mass produced, and we need relationship with Christ, not a program, to be fully alive. Perhaps I will write my own self a letter to remind me all over again. Remember: you are happier here and God is enough.

I have supper dishes to clean up, prayers to pray, tears to cry, holy daily work to do. Joy comes in the morning hand in hand with whatever may come. Glory to God.

STRIPTEASE

Sheila Seiler Lagrand

F YOU WERE TO LOOK AT A TIMELINE OF MY LIFE," I confessed to my friend, "and someone asked you to review all the events and choose the time when I became depressed, right now is *not* the moment you would circle."

"I've started seeing a spiritual director," she replied. "We meet once a month. And she's taught me this: Even people like me, who have a really good, normal childhood? We all pick up splinters as we go through life. And we all get our toes stepped on. Now normally, a stepped-on toe isn't a big deal. But when that stepped-on toe carries a splinter that's been festering for years and years . . ." Her voice trailed off, point made.

"Truthfully," I said, "I've been going back, trying to remember a time when I was happy. I've worked my way back to 1987 and I haven't found it yet." I hoped my friend would head me off at the pass, turn our conversation in a lighter direction, comment on the weather. I picked up my coffee mug, wrapped both hands around its warmth and inhaled the dark aroma as if it could comfort me.

She sat, silent, offering an encouraging smile.

I took a deep breath and leaned back in my chair, focused on a tree growing on the far bank of the river.

"My high school was on top of a hill. The road down that hill was winding and had some strange banks to it. Eight of my classmates died in car accidents going down that hill during my high school years.

"I remember when I was sixteen, driving the family car down that hill one night, wanting to floor the accelerator, head off the side of the road, just . . . be done." I took a deep breath. "I've never said that out loud before."

My friend nodded, waiting. I waited too. *Really?* I thought. *You're not going to talk me back from this edge? I don't want to share this.*

A bird whistled somewhere downriver.

I have to share this.

"Well," I finally said. "I'm ready for more coffee. Are you?" I rose.

At lunchtime in the retreat center's dining hall, I saw her scanning the room as I entered. She patted the seat beside hers, smiling.

It was a revelation. She did not turn away; in fact she sought me. I nearly collapsed, staggered by the stack of truths piling up on me:

You hide. You're always hiding.

You keep people at arm's length. You don't let them close enough to really see you.

You think if people knew the real you, they'd be disgusted. Or filled with pity. Or both.

You wear that stinking mask all the time. Even yesterday, when you first arrived at this long-awaited retreat, finally, finally gathering with your blog friends in real life—even then, even though they knew you were depressed, your voice was too bright. Your jokes flew too fast. You laughed like a braying mule.

You're people lazy, that's what you are. It's easy to relate through writing, where you can ponder every word, revise before you share. But in real life, in real time, you're intimidated. Thoughtless words could slip out. You might hurt someone.

Someone might hurt you. You might cry. You might scream. You might show your belly—that pale flesh that never sees the sunshine.

I'm chewing absently, smiling, nodding, acting engaged in the conversation. Acting. I shake my head.

I didn't come here to act.

After the meal, another friend comes beside me gently murmuring, "How are you doing?"

"I just caught myself," I say. "I've been putting on the act, laughing, joking, smiling like everything is great."

"You don't have to," she says. "This is a safe place. You are loved."

The quick tears ambush me. I blink rapidly, search my pocket for a tissue.

"I've been thinking," I tell her as we sit on a bench. "I hide too much. I don't want to let people get close. I'm more comfortable writing than sitting and having a conversation. I'd rather text than call even."

"It sounds to me," she says slowly, refusing to let my gaze wander from her face, "like you've been listening to the enemy. Look at me," she barks, as I study my hands. "Look. At. Me."

She stares me down. "You've been thinking that you're too wrapped up in yourself with this depression thing, haven't you? That you should just be counting your blessings and serving others and worshiping? That you have a husband who loves you and a family who cares and a nice home and a job and food and decent health and what on earth do you have to be sad about?

You're thinking that your problems—your pain—you—aren't worth your friends' time. That's what you're thinking, right? That's why you laugh so hard and crack so many jokes, isn't it?"

I nod dumbly, mesmerized.

"Those are lies." She bites at the words, fierce. "It's *not* wrong for you to want to feel better. And yes, you *can* be sad and grateful at the same time. Listen to me. Listen. It is right to care for yourself. It is right to let your friends know that you're hurting. It's okay to be weak. God loves you. He certainly didn't command you to love your neighbors as poorly as you love yourself, did he?

"I've been where you are. Life can be better. But you have to believe that you weren't destined to carry this load of hurt on your walk through the world. Take your medicine, yes. Rest, yes. Surround yourself with people you love, yes.

"*It's not a sin to want to be well.*"

She stops, spent, breathing hard as if she's run down the path beside the river. I struggle to identify an odd sound that I suddenly hear.

It is me, sobbing.

My friend wraps her arms around me, rocking gently. She doesn't let go. And her rocking, my other friend's chair-patting and nodding, the listening, the not turning away, they teach me something.

All my life, I've offered up some feeble striptease to people who love me. *Here's a peek at me. See? I'm uncovering myself—but you only get a glimpse.*

My beautiful friends who met me far from home along the banks of a slow, undulating Texas river have taught me the first truth I need to be well, to become whole:

I am not obscene. It's okay to let you see me.

WITHOUT PEOPLE LIKE YOU

Sarah Markley

EARLY ON, I BEGAN TO UNDERSTAND just how much of a liability it is to be sensitive.

When I was in grade school the boy I liked was the boy all the girls liked. He wasn't tall, but he was tan and confident. He charmed both teachers and lunch ladies alike and was caught holding hands with Julie in the fourth grade. I was nothing like Julie. She was tiny and petite, had long, curly, blonde hair and giggled at jokes. I was big and too loud, my brown hair was greasy, and I always felt exposed and alone in crowds. Maybe it's why I liked Nate so much—he was independent and confident when I was not. Nate didn't have to rely on his mother to drive him to and from school. He rode his BMX—the premier sign of a ten-year-old who'd cut apron strings early.

And I was in love.

Or at least really strong *like*.

He left our school after fifth grade, and the playground just wasn't the same without him.

That first fall when the sixth graders become the alphas in the lunch line and on the playground, I began to feel better, like I could maybe be cool someday. Maybe. I got a cute, in-style-for-the-times haircut (which, looking back, I now know was a bad, bi-level, part-shag, feathered mess), and I started wearing makeup.

After school one day in October I heard that Nate had ridden his bike to campus to see his old friends. I fluttered and faltered and ran with the other girls to where he'd ridden up.

All the boys were messing around with him, all the girls were standing in little huddles nearby, and Nate was glorious. He was brown from the summer, his dark hair had gotten even longer now, and he emitted a cool vibe that would have put Tom Cruise to shame. He rolled up on his BMX and came to a stop behind the multipurpose room, surrounded by the boys and some of the more forward, less nervous girls.

It was very strong *like* all over again. I left my friends and walked up to him.

"Hey Nate, remember me?" He slowly turned from his friends, a wide smile fading slightly.

"Hey." He cocked his head a little, arms still resting on his bike, two feet planted on the ground astride it.

"I got my hair cut." I gestured at my hideous feathered bob-shag. And then, for me, time itself began to slow to a horrible creep.

"Oh." And he walked his bike to where the rest of the boys had withdrawn.

Ouch.

The tears burned in my eyes. I left my friends, walked quickly to get my book bag and found my mother in the car, my sister already waiting, to pick me up from school. I'd never known embarrassment or shame quite like that before.

It was such a simple thing but so significant. When I think about that grade school crush, I don't think about *him* necessarily, but I think about that autumn afternoon when he rode up on his bike and I made a fool of myself.

I've always felt embarrassed of my feelings because they come so strong and brilliant. I never knew anything different (because we all only really *know* what we *are*) but as I grew, I looked around and watched my friends easily get "over" boyfriend breakups and friendship breakups. I began to wonder if anyone was like me. I was envious of all the people around me as they just brushed things off.

I've been labeled sensitive, overly sensitive and even hypersensitive. I could never get over heartache or snubs; I loved people big but subsequently would get my feelings deeply hurt several times a day. The idea of letting something "roll off my back" was almost an impossibility to me. I just didn't know how.

When I was in middle school I met a male youth leader who had trouble speaking anything without a sarcastic drip to his tone. If the "that's what she said" meme had been invented then, he would have been a major perpetrator. There was nothing sexually inappropriate about Dwayne and his relationships with the kids in my youth group, but he couldn't have a conversation without innumerable put-downs, constant negative comments and an all-around arrogance.

"Why are you so sensitive, Sarah?"

"Can't you take a joke?"

"What's wrong with you, gonna CRY?"

He was every bit a bully. Dwayne was in his late twenties, and the kids he was bullying were fifteen years younger than him. And when a bully bullies, you begin to believe what he says about you: that you are weak and a crybaby and that your feelings are somehow holding you back.

If I could have cut out the sensitive part of my heart, I would have.

I've never believed that my sensitive heart was something that was beneficial. Even though my parents seemed to roll with the punches of my raw mood swings, my tender heart had gotten me into a lot of heartache early on with crushes and with friends. Being sensitive was always a bad thing but something I could at least live with. Maybe someday I'd feel less tender?

However, until I met Dwayne, I'd never been bullied about it.

He was right about one thing: it just wasn't cool to be sensitive. He wasn't the only person who helped hammer into my brain and my heart that the big love and big hurt of a tender heart is a liability and not an asset. I would meet many others: boys I would date, girls I would befriend, people I would work with someday.

Big hearts get hurt easily.

Big hearts get broken.

Tender feelings are signs of weakness.

I slowly learned to hide my heart. With each unkind word that dug in deep and every time I was called "too sensitive," I also learned how to build walls to protect a big, open heart.

I kept a secret, though. I hoped that someday, someone might love me because of my sensitive heart and not despite it.

More than twenty years later my therapist discovered my secret wish, and like all good therapists do, she drew those thoughts and feelings out of me.

"But your sensitivity *is* an asset, Sarah." She smiled at me from across the tiny counseling room. "Don't you understand?"

I let out a big sigh in disbelief. I was so far removed from the bare soul of me, the part of me that might believe that the tenderness was a good thing, and I'd built up so many walls to hide it that I shook my head.

"I don't see how."

I told her the story of Dwayne and all the others that I had allowed to bully my heart.

"Tender people can take the emotional temperature of a room in a way that no one else can," she began. "Sensitive people can see the feelings in a conversation in brilliant color, and they are skilled at understanding other people's hearts. Without people like you, Sarah, there would be no empathy in the world."

I was thirty-seven, and she was the first person in my life who had recognized my sensitivity as beautiful and who believed it was something to be proud of.

What I am learning, as I stare down forty in the face, is that I was born to be tender. Every person who tries to bully that out of me and every word that tries to create a callus over a raw place stands in the face of the God who intentionally created this sensitive heart. And when I try to protect my own heart by building up strong walls of apathy to guard myself, I'm telling God he's done a bad job with me.

I'm at my most confident when I own up to who God has made me to be.

My oldest daughter, eleven right now, has this same brilliantly big-feeling heart. She loves and cries and hurts and cries and it is all too familiar.

In the past year I've begun to change my parenting language from "don't cry" to "let's figure out an appropriate response to this." I never want to be the bully of her heart, but to teach her tenderly that there are beneficial and detrimental ways to approach situa-tions. I never want her to feel as if crying is a crime. It simply isn't.

Crying disarms people. It can be ugly and sometimes it's a mirror into the deep side of human emotion that is sometimes hard to look at. But even so, true weeping is a sign of deep emotion, and that isn't wrong.

One evening after a particularly difficult day I crawled into bed with her as she cried softly.

"You're special," I told her.

"Why?" She scowled, sniffled and turned her head back toward the wall. She was so upset about something trivial to me but very big to her.

"Because you understand how people feel. You have a special heart with special tools to understand the big, hard feelings of your friends because you feel things big and hard yourself."

I don't know if she believed me, but I'm going to keep speaking these things to her, keep putting that into her head, because someday she'll have a Nate. And he'll care about his friends and his bike more than her, and it will hurt.

And she might have a Dwayne who will bully her. He'll be sarcastic, and he will make her feel small and weak. She'll question God about why he made her this way. Maybe it was a mistake.

But maybe by the time she finds her Nate and her Dwayne she'll have enough confidence to stand up and say no. Maybe she'll understand that her heart was created with just enough tenderness to love the world as it needs to be loved and to feel the hurts of others so that she can mourn with those who mourn. And maybe she can accept that her heart was made to be both sensitive and strong, brilliant and hopeful, and full of empathy for a broken world.

THE CHOREOGRAPHY OF GOD

Holly Grantham

I WAKE EARLY IN THE MORNING, when the world is at its darkest. At that hour, the stars are still twinkling, and among the quiet, you can hear them humming. In these suspended moments, the ones stretched between slumber and doing, there resides a holy knowing, and I ache to feel its pulse and fall in line with the rhythm. It won't be long before the sun cracks open the sky and the rushing tide of children and appointments and duties surges in on its wake. So, it is here, in this juncture of time, where I begin the slow process of revealing.

It hasn't always been this way. For so very long, I only scribbled down my thoughts in secret spaces, the kind hidden between hard sleeves of blank books, the ones whose fanciful and ornate covers stood in stark contradiction to the thoughts inside. What I wrote on those pages didn't seem fit for this world. They were more the babblings of my heart and mind, in rabid conversation with each other, and full of more questions than answers, more torment than realization. No, those words flowed from dark corners and were smeared with doubt. They read more like desperate prayers wreathed with bile, and they couldn't possibly serve any good to anyone else, not even, perhaps, to the angst-ridden adolescent that penned them. Those ramblings needed to stay hidden.

Then, years later, I pulled out one of those old journals. As I read through the sporadic entries I was struck at how time and distance from the words had shaped them into something completely different than they had seemed at their conception. What before had been a slew of sprawling words wrought with raw emotion and little sense had, in time, taken on new forms laced with insight and conviction. At the time of their writing, I had been so caught up in the moment and so desperate to grab hold of what was happening in and around me that I hadn't bothered to stop and self-edit. I had, quite simply, bled on the page, and I had allowed the white space to collect my wounded flow of words. A new reading unveiled something revolutionary: the act of writing had revealed the hidden.

Before my discovery, I had never been one to wax poetic in mixed company. I shied from public debate. If there was conflict, I hid. And if I ever did decide that I actually had an opinion on something, I wrapped it securely in self-doubt and condemnation. I lived with the belief that what I thought about the world and its goings on was of little consequence to the great conversation. I was small and simple and silent. The universe was better and prettier and smarter without my piddling contributions.

But when I read those written words of mine, I could no longer reconcile what lay before me with my previous loathsome dismissals. When I spilled deep on the page, far reaching ripples emerged. And with each new ring of words came connection—

between my head and my heart. It began to appear that maybe, just maybe, writing was a kind of prayer language for me. Perhaps, when first conceived, it was as if the words swam and shook on the page. But then, in the baring of them, all stripped and naked, the rustling of the Holy Spirit spun them into something more, something rich and golden. The words took on flesh and bore life.

If this writing, this partnering in creation, was to mean anything beyond my own soul, it needed to be brought into the light. I needed to bring others into that intimacy. So I began to write with the intention of sharing. And it was frightful and painful and beautiful all at once. As I let the Holy Spirit into my caves of darkness I felt things begin to break loose. I became aware of the choreography of God. Where I bent and swayed, God held me fast and secure. As I explored the spaces in between I discovered that those places are full of all that has come before and all that is to unfold, and such a space is holy.

These days, writing is not just a discipline or something I practice. It is spiritual. It is sacrifice. It is me, laying bare on the page all that I am or hope to be, praying that my dross might be redeemed. I sang out a broken hallelujah when I stumbled upon this from Henri Nouwen:

> Writing is a process in which we discover what lives in us. The deepest satisfaction of writing is precisely that it opens up new spaces within us of which we were not aware before we started to write. To write is to embark on a journey whose final destination we do not know. Thus, writing requires a real act of trust. We have to say to ourselves: "I do not yet know what I carry in my heart, but I trust that it will emerge as I write." Writing is like giving away the few

loaves and fishes one has, trusting that they will multiply in the giving. Once we dare to "give away" on paper the few thoughts that come to us, we start discovering how much is hidden underneath these thoughts and gradually come in touch with our own riches.

I continue to submit myself to the process, daily. It is both exhausting and life giving, but it is also transformative. I spent a long time hoarding the few loaves and fishes that I believed were mine to keep, but I now realize that to hold back that meager meal is to forfeit the feast to which it leads. Now, every morning, I choose anew to follow the advice of Anne Sexton and "put [my] ear down close to [my] soul and listen hard." Such leaning in deep sometimes feels like falling, and many days, the soul is quiet and broody, but still, I lean. For in the bowing down low and listening, there is a banquet to be had. And I am hungry.

REDEMPTION LOOKS BEAUTIFUL ON YOU

Shelly Miller

I'T'S ONE OF THOSE EVENINGS before the humidity suffocates in the South. A group of friends gather after dinner for dessert on my back porch. I sit barefoot among men in Bermudas, women in flowing strapless dresses, our French manicured toes huddled together like a prayer before the next play. Voices filter through porch screens into the still ebony, and for a few moments we listen to the cacophony of chirping crickets in the stillness. I expose a part of my past like a chapter in the middle of a book revealing an unexpected twist.

We're spouses and coworkers, ministry partners talking about mistakes before marriage among half-empty glasses of red wine, crumpled napkins and crumby plates. Laughing about the era of bad hair and fashion styles, regret over relationships and how we managed to win the heart of our spouse. It's when someone admits smoking marijuana that I lean over to my husband and smile.

"I bet no one has ever grown marijuana in their backyard," I whisper in his ear.

He laughs and challenges the couples with a question to see if anyone actually went that far in their rebellious days of youth. "How many of you grew marijuana in your backyard?" he jokes. I'm the only one that raises my hand.

Ruckus laughter transforms to silent stares, their mouths drawn open like baby birds in the nest waiting for more. They remind me that my life is not common, though raising my hand felt that way.

"Well, *I* didn't actually grow it in my backyard," I admit, breaking the rhythm of the cricket choir. "It was a relative and her live-in girlfriend who grew it."

This twisted puzzle piece with jagged edges I've held up, it doesn't fit into the picture they see of a pastor's wife who shops at Loft and lives in a middle-class neighborhood of manicured mania. So I fill in the holes.

I tell them about growing up around promiscuous lesbians during my teen years, how they grew marijuana in the empty overgrown acreage that once fed horses behind our rental house. I remember the leaves drying on paper towels in the sunny kitchen window, admit to hiding in my bedroom when cars made their way down our bumpy gravel road pushing dust up to the crown of trees, holding passengers with pockets full of money.

I tell them about passing familiar faces in school hallways the morning after I watched them smoke pot through the crack in my bedroom door. I tell them that I resent Lynyrd Skynyrd and Ted Nugent for keeping me up all those school nights, and the way Johnny Carson's voice lulled me to sleep in peace. I tell them that my mother's alcoholism creates a wall of stifling silence between us, now and for the past sixteen years.

"You're a miracle," one of them responds. "Actually, it's a miracle you two got married," he waxes honest with a smile.

A miracle? Those words dangle on the thick air for a few moments. I think about how I knew my husband was the most eligible bachelor in our megachurch before I met him. A recent college graduate from architectural school, living in a prestigious part of Phoenix with parents of notable reputation. And he asks *me*, the young woman raised by a single mother with cockroaches coming out of her walls, to marry him two months after our first date in his hometown. Perhaps that *is* a miracle.

A few days later, one of those back-porch friends trades her sundress for jeans and calls a babysitter to meet me for lunch. We exchange small talk over square plates of radish flowers and sip lemon water, watching suits in sunglasses scurry past the floor-to-ceiling window where we're seated.

As she stares out the window, squinting into sun bouncing off the hoods of parked cars, she reveals a discarded piece of her story to complete the puzzle of friendship we've worked on together over the past few months. She admits that her father was an alcoholic when she was a child. Then she tells me about a pilgrimage toward inner healing, one she thought was over until recent circumstances with a sibling put her back on the journey.

Her sister chooses emotional distance as the way to cope with a disagreement over church politics and she struggles to get past feelings of rejection. Revisiting her childhood all over again, she's guilt-ridden about the crumbs lying on a floor she thought was swept clean. The enemy of the soul takes the white-glove test and accuses her of leaving dirt in corners she couldn't reach.

"You know we continue circling around the same issues where we were most wounded in our lives," I tell her. "Salvation is an ongoing process. The circle just gets smaller with every visit."

She takes a bite of her fish taco, wipes her mouth on the napkin and looks up at me like finding the string hanging on a light bulb screwed into the ceiling of a dark room. "Really? You think so?" she asks. I nod the affirmative. "That makes me feel better."

I fidget with my cell phone when she excuses herself to the restroom. When she sits back down to a cleared table, I hear those familiar words again. "You're a miracle, you know?" she says.

It's something I've grown used to hearing, like my children calling me Mom. And while I often think miracles look more like raising the dead back to life or healing the lame to walk again, I'm accepting the reality that miracles happen in the everyday choice that believes in the power of redemption more than our failure and pain.

On the drive back home, revelation strikes me at the stoplight. I wouldn't be sharing this middle-of-the-day conversation with my girlfriend if I hadn't revealed that warped puzzle piece of my story on that steamy evening. And perhaps this is where the beauty of redemption begins, in releasing the ugly parts of our story held captive by shame.

YOU'RE NOT ALONE

Holley Gerth

WE'RE CIRCLED IN AN UPSTAIRS ROOM, leaning back on comfortable couches. The smooth leather speaks of having it all together. We're careful not to set our cups too close to the edge of the coffee table.

But somehow we start being messy with our hearts.

One of my friends speaks bravely first. She shares a struggle in her marriage. We nod in understanding because we've been there too.

We tell the stories of what happens when no one is looking.

We dare to whisper what we sometimes wonder.

We look each other in the eyes and the soul.

Finally I pipe up and confess my previous struggle with depression. Someone says, "I never would have guessed that about you." That response means a lot to me because it reminds me of what God has done in my life—how he has turned depression from a place where I live to somewhere I only occasionally visit. That's miraculous to me because that journey was anything but simple. It held many nights of staring at the ceiling, long conversations, wrestling prayers, letting go, giving up and being found all over again.

But her response also tugs at my heart because it's a reminder of how often I forget to talk about the hard in my life. I don't remember how much I need to share, how the light of conversation can slip into our dark corners and make them beautiful again. So in this moment I pause and find words to go back to where I once was and retrace the hard steps, the ones that helped make me who I am today.

I'm independent by nature. My mom still tells the now-legendary story of how, on the first day of kindergarten, I wouldn't let her take me to school. Instead I climbed on the bus. All. By. Myself.

And I still tend to do the same sometimes.

Facing depression . . . All. By. Myself.

Tackling a new project . . . All. By. Myself.

Conquering a fear . . . All. By. Myself.

I don't know what that is in me, in us. Perhaps it feels vulnerable to share, to ask for help. But I'm learning, slowly, that we are not made for All. By. Myself. We pay a high price when we choose to live that way. C. S. Lewis said:

> Love anything and your heart will certainly be wrung and possibly broken. If you want to make sure of keeping it intact you must give it to no one, not even an animal. Wrap it carefully round with hobbies and little luxuries; avoid all entanglements. Lock it up safe in the casket or coffin of your selfishness. But in that casket, safe, dark, motionless, airless, it will change. It will not be broken; it will become unbreakable, impenetrable, irredeemable. To love is to be vulnerable.

Our need for each other goes all the way back to the Garden when God said it wasn't good for man to be alone. *Before the fall.* So our need for each other isn't an imperfection. It's part of the perfect plan.

Our souls need to circle up on couches, to climb in the car for the ride to school, to put our fingers to the keyboard and tell the people who love us how we're *really* doing. I shared this recently on my blog:

> The reason why I write the way I do is because I need to hear it too.
>
> Because sometimes I forget I'm loved.
>
> Some nights it's hard to wait for dawn.
>
> Some moments I struggle to be strong.
>
> *I write what I need to remember.* Words are the trail markers I leave on the journey of life so I can say, *"Oh, yes, I've passed this way before. Now I know how to move past this place again."*
>
> I've struggled with depression.
>
> I was once diagnosed with social anxiety.
>
> I've walked the valleys.
>
> It's not where I live now. But I've been there. *And sometimes I go back.*
>
> Don't we all?
>
> I forget to tell you that sometimes—to say that if you ever get the idea I have it all together you shouldn't believe it. *That I sweat and cry the ugly cry and have dust bunnies and bad hair days and I whine and I sometimes completely forget that I'm already amazing.*
>
> I write to find my way home.
>
> I write to reconnect with Love.

I write to know I'm not alone. *And because of you, I'm not.*

Thanks for sharing the journey with me. In case you didn't know, I appreciate you even more than words can convey. I'm glad we're in this together.

Just as we are.

And not yet all we will be.

Our best is still ahead.

That post led to comments like this one:

> I could have written this post too. Thank you for letting me know I'm not the only one who struggles with these things. Sometimes it's hard to admit that to each other. But we need to say it out loud so we can help each other and God can heal us.

Unexpected voices from all over the world saying, "You're not alone. You don't have to do this all by yourself."

Who do you need to hear that from today?

Who needs to hear it from you?

By the end of our time together that evening, my friends and I had all revealed a struggle. We'd shared something else just as important too. *Laughter.* There's a certain kind of laughter that comes in those moments. It's part relief and all joy. It's what you feel when your heart feels at home, when you stop being All. By. Yourself.

That's the real secret: joy comes from community, from connection. It spills out from the places we think we have to keep locked up inside. It finds its voice in two little words, "You too?" For when those words are spoken we remember this: we're human.

That simple truth means that we will always need to sit on couches and share our souls. We will always need to send honest emails. We will always need to connect over cups of coffee. We will always be messy and broken and beautiful too.

We descended the stairs that evening with lighter hearts. We stood a little taller and smiled a little wider.

I stepped out into the brilliant evening.

All. By. Myself.

And yet, looking at the scattered stars and thinking of the Maker of them, I had a new understanding of how none of us are ever really alone.

GRAVITY

Emily P. Freeman

I'T'S SATURDAY, AND THE HOUSE and I have a rare few moments together. My husband is out, the kids are with friends and I am alone in the midst of these walls we painted yellow and call home.

I sit with the last few pages of a book I'm reading, close it up and feel like crying. I can't place the reason for the tears, but they don't surprise me.

Quietness does this, allows space for the deep longings of my soul to rise up and mingle with the daily worries of my life. I would rather not face them, so my hands begin to twitch, looking for something to accomplish. I long to be still but also am aware of the dirty dishes and the floor that needs vacuumed. I am caught between the physical and the invisible and know I need to make a choice.

I decide to linger in the emotion of the moment, to let the tears lead me to what is really going on. Life is going fairly well these days—we have our health, our home, some friends and enough food. Still, I'm aware of a dull ache, a deep knowing that I long for more than family and good health. It feels selfish to admit that.

The book I was reading sits face down on the table. On my knees now, aware of God and my joints, I bend down low and touch my face to the carpet. Closing my eyes to ignore the crumbs, I feel my heart beat in my ears, the earth pull my skin to the ground.

We don't notice gravity when we're right side up. It all feels normal until we spin it around the wrong way. It's only when we get upside down that we feel the pull, the dragging down, the lifting toward the ground like a weight.

Turn me upside down. Let me see God.

A series of images come to mind as I consider my life up to this point. I am a woman who spent many years denying my frail humanity. I used to see life as a line straight up, every accomplishment, hurt and victory getting me one rung closer to maturity and contentment. I thought that as I grew older, I would grow wiser. And to me, wisdom meant I wouldn't cry over invisible longing or have to contend with a restless awareness of my own inadequacies. When you have everything you need, what is there left to long for?

I have a lot of practice ignoring the state of my soul. I have pushed it away with locked elbows and up-turned face.

I have resented the dripping neediness, the crouching coward.

I have quieted the burning desires.

I have neutralized, softened, muzzled for the sake of appearances. When my twins were first born, I had the home, the children, the husband, the good life. But I couldn't bear the thought of revealing how inadequate I felt as a mother, how desperate I felt as wife, how deeply I longed for true friends to share my burdens.

I didn't intend to hide, but when a glimpse of weakness would peek out to the world, it was too uncomfortable. When I couldn't hide it, I would try to fix it. When I couldn't fix it, I would try to rationalize it. When I couldn't change myself, that's when I began to break.

While the breaking of the rebel may come with alarms and blaring lights, attention-getting interventions, and phone calls in the night, the breaking of the vanilla comes as a silent crack in the soul, an understanding of our deep selfishness in the midst of our deep woundedness. There wasn't one particular moment of transformation, one event that opened my eyes. Mine was a silent breaking. The cracks and fissures were gradual and without fanfare.

I slowly had to face the reality of what I was doing. I was trying hard to live life the right way, holding on to my rules-y religion, soaring with pride when I got it right, shrinking in shame when I failed. I had to face this cycle and name it in the presence of Jesus—this is the self-life, the all-about-me life, the flesh disguised by sweet smiles and twisted intentions.

Don't let the mask fool you. This kind of living is sin.

It sounds reasonable to say I needed healing from this try-hard life, but I know my own capabilities. I know my wounds, though real and not always my fault, are simply catalysts in shaping my own unique version of the flesh.

The wounds didn't cause my dysfunction. I was born with a dysfunctional soul, and my wounds simply serve to show it up.

I don't just need healing. I need *forgiveness*.

I wear my scars on the inside, but I'm done denying they are there. Now I face them as they are, turn them over in the presence of God, allow him to see my need and meet me where I am, not where I think I should be.

Today, as I kneel down on my dirty carpet, I am aware of my desperate need for him and I dare not shy away from it. I practice the art of "allowing that which is usually unknown and unnamed within me to surface" (as Ruth Haley Barton so eloquently says it). There are happenings and movements of the soul that cannot be explained or outlined. I'm learning to accept the day and the life story as it has been, full of disappointment as well as delight, but never able to give more than it was designed to give.

When I finally decide to bare the soul, I know *the soul isn't bare*. As I kneel down low, I see the mess for what it is. But beneath that, I also see the shadow of a woman who is fully alive with desire, a desire so deep that to face it feels upside down. There is a heart of flesh underneath that stone façade; a warm, beating passion, fully alive underneath the calculated well-laid plans. In moments like these, I face my true self once again. I remember anew how resurrection life only comes after death and how the self-life will never satisfy.

I remember as I am bowed down low, gravity pulling my weight to the ground: *I wasn't made for health, for the blessed life, for the abundant goodness of the small gifts.*

It no longer surprises me when I feel ungracious in the midst of abundance.

I practice gratitude, but my dissatisfaction ought not force me immediately into shame. Instead, let it lead me to understand my true desire—to know God as he is, and so to know myself.

The people and blessings of this earthly life are enjoyable and fulfilling to an extent, but I have to be careful not to put them in a place they were not meant for. I am thankful for the gifts, but I don't want to expect them, and I never want to be surprised when they don't fully satisfy. These gifts are my reminders, but they are not the whole.

Standing up, dizziness wins for a moment, turning the room black. I reach out for the back of the chair and wait for the room to show up again. When it does, I notice my still hands and dry face.

They'll be home soon. The house is still a mess, and in many ways so is my soul. I have journeyed down into the true source of my desire, and now I am returning. I pray that these few minutes of sacred work, the work of knowing and of being known, will not be quickly forgotten.

May this invisible redemption show up visible on this ordinary Saturday in the house with the yellow walls.

BREATHING FRESH AIR

Mandy Steward

THINK I HAVE YOGA TO THANK for saving my faith," I said to a new friend of mine as I rode home in her car, minutes after experiencing my first meditation class with her.

We were discussing Christians, which my friend does not call herself, and we were discussing Buddhists, which the lady that led our meditation class was, and we were discussing yoga and how many Christians are leery of partaking in the practice.

We sat together in a small yoga studio by the railroad tracks listening to a smiling, soft-spoken woman with a shaved head, dressed in Buddhist robes. She explained the altar she had set up beside her on a tiny little table, and I realized how much my view of God had expanded in one year.

Exactly a year ago to the day, I had been in Dallas on a three-day trip with my husband, celebrating our tenth anniversary. I was also, for the record, feeling fairly stagnant in my faith. We stumbled on a huge used bookstore, and both of us being book lovers, we felt as though we had landed in an undiscovered paradise of musty books and yellowed pages.

I soon found myself in the philosophy section, browsing through a book titled *The World of Zen* by Nancy Wilson Ross. The book felt good in my hands. Its cover was pliable and well loved, pages dense with quality paper, little cursive notes dotting the margins, drawn there by a previous reader. I browsed the words. These quotes stood out to me:

> I do not need to burn the Gospels in order to read Hui-Neng. —Hubert Benoit

> As thou knowest not what is the way of the spirit, nor how the bones do grow in the womb of her that is with child: even so thou knowest not the works of God who maketh all. (Eccles 11:5 KJV)

I was intrigued. I read more words, glancing over the top of the cover, back and forth to see if anyone was looking at me. I felt a bit of a maverick. My heartbeats quickened. I closed the cover and tucked the book under my arm. I was going to walk out of this store with a book about Zen. I felt as if I was a one-year-old birthday baby tasting sugar for the first time. Was I really allowed to put my hands into this gooey icing? Was I really allowed to get messy in the layers of this beautiful cake? Was I really free to explore and smash it all over my face if I so desired?

Hours later, laying poolside at our hotel, I began digging into the paragraphs of the unknown. I found myself shocked as I actually related to the story of the Siddartha Gautama (whom we know as Buddha), a young man who went searching secretly, outside of his family's palace gates, for answers to the haunting questions of what to do with death and disease and the hungry and homeless. A young man determined to find a way to live with himself despite the obvious darkness that existed on the outskirts of what everyone liked to believe was safe.

The more I read, the more my faith swelled with hope and a new vitality. I might as well have been that freshly baptized little girl sitting on a small-town Ohio curb one Easter Sunday, brimming with the desire to share my faith with anyone who passed by. I was coming to life again.

Days unfolded into months and I found myself more and more drawn to this Eastern philosophy. I became saturated in all things yoga, meditation and mindfulness. I liked the way this Zen element to my faith was allowing for lights and darks to co-mingle in my life. My negative emotions weren't taboo. There was a place for them.

Shortly after I finished reading the Zen book, I bought my first yoga DVD. It seemed like a natural progression. I started regularly attending yoga classes at the YMCA. After my second class, a woman introduced herself and encouraged me to stick with it. She gave me a lot of positive feedback and then talked about what yoga meant to her. I appreciated her insight and told her that more than anything I hoped that what I learned in yoga would transfer off the mat.

"I need to learn to breathe through my intense life, just like I breathe through an intense class," I told her.

She gave me a look of complete understanding and said, "So do I, honey. So do I."

In many facets of our faith, it is helpful to have an outer expression of our inner beliefs. We may get baptized. We may take Communion. We may kneel to pray. We may lift our arms up in worship. It is part of our mind-body-soul connection. Yoga has become a physical expression for me of my faith. A way to physically practice letting things go.

As I follow what I believe to be the promptings of the Spirit of God inside of me, I find myself exploring all sorts of new territory. What I am learning on my mat in yoga is transferring to how I enter into these new mysteries of my faith. I bend a little in my mind, as far as I feel comfortable, and then I breathe and see if I feel as though I can safely release muscles to allow myself to go even deeper or if I am at my proverbial edge, needing to back off.

I call this my "walking on the ceiling mentality." It's my way of starting to see the world with new eyes by living an upside-down life. My perspective on everything is changing. I'm tweaking screwy philosophies and tearing down barriers left and right as I discover new truths of God.

I never felt uncomfortable while sitting in the Buddhist meditation class with my friend. At no point did I wonder whether I was compromising my faith to be there. In fact, during one part of her lecture, I considered how absolutely similar this felt to women's Bible studies I have attended in the past. There we were, a small intimate group of women, all lined up on our fold-out chairs, listening to an older woman share her wisdom.

At one point she asked us to close our eyes and to breathe deep. She suggested that as we inhaled we imagine that we were breathing in light, and as we exhaled we were breathing out thick black smoke. We felt light come in and we felt dark flow out. It was an even exchange. We recognized the presence of both. We judged neither. This is the yin yang I've heard tell of. This is the reason an artist must sketch both shadows and illuminations in order to get a realistic interpretation.

I feel deeply aware of both my lights and my darks; the inhales and the exhales are a familiar flow. I am so relieved that the black smoke is finally given a place to exist. I can go there and not be smothered by it because I'm going there with intention. I'm going there with others. I'm going there with a humbling awareness of all that I am and all that I am not. I breathe out the darkness and follow it up by a thick, long inhale of light. When God feels estranged or dangerous or non-existent, when the questions outweigh the answers, when the weight of living is heavier than I care to admit, all I have is my breath, and that can actually be enough.

After the meditation ended, she asked us how we did. She looked directly at me and said, "Well, what did you think?"

"I honestly wondered if I was going to open my eyes and find the whole room filled with all my black smoke." I laughed. Everyone else did as well. I knew they understood.

"I was hoping I wasn't going to hear the women beside me start coughing. I was so relieved to hear you say at one point that the black smoke was rising up into the sky and dissipating. I'm glad it has a place to go."

I no longer feel like I'm exploiting God by admitting the black smoke exists. I no longer feel ashamed when I'm wanting to wave my arms around in it a bit to see what it's made of.

I am using the physical aspects of yoga to learn the mental practices of dying to self. I no longer freak out when my ego gets a bit miffed and begins to hiss at me: *You're being too vulnerable. You're veering off the proper religious path. You're slipping and falling a bit too much and it's getting embarrassing.*

I am learning to listen and trust myself and thereby also the power and love of God within. I am learning to monitor a sort of internal flexibility and to back off whenever I personally feel too much strain. The question I keep coming back to is, "Am I still able to breathe deeply?" If I can, then I know I'm safe in the dark place, the mysterious place, the place that I, as an artist, simply must explore in order to make some sort of peace between the interweaving destinies of humanity and divinity.

LOOK AT ME, DADDY!

Dan King

WHEN I WAS IN MY LATE TWENTIES, I decided to get serious about this God and church thing. Once I did, I was fully committed to the mission of the church. I was one of those guys who refused to be out-served. My wife and I had just gotten married, and the first thing we decided to do as a newlywed couple was to volunteer with our church's youth group. We jumped on almost every opportunity that came up to serve. Serving was important to me because I believed that it was important to God. Over the years, I've served in the youth group, led small group studies, led the twentysomethings' ministry, taught in vacation Bible school, served on the board of directors, taught in the school of ministry and organized major (and minor) outreach events. And that's just for starters.

At some point I also decided that I needed to learn too. I started taking classes in our local Bible college and eventually went on to a larger college to begin my studies in theology. And this all happened in my "free" time outside of my full-time job and the half a dozen ministry opportunities that I was involved with at any given time. Where serving gave me a physical outlet for my faith, studying gave me an intellectual outlet.

Then I caught the missions bug, and now I'm taking a couple of mission trips every year and leading teams of other bloggers on trips to experience the work being done in these far-away communities and then write about it for their audiences. The stories are just too good and important to not be told.

Even this description of what I do doesn't seem to hold a light to what my life of lay ministry has been like. I've had friends over and over say to me, "Dude, I don't know how you do it all!" And others would totally validate me by saying things like, "You're an inspiration," and, "You're living the Christian life like all of us should be living it!"

Like I said, I work hard. And I couldn't imagine doing this faith thing any other way.

ASKING WHY

The more I studied the Word, the more I thought that this must be the kind of life that pleases God. I think about James who taught us that faith without works is dead. I'm not some kind of works-only extremist, but I hear the heart of this first-century pastor who teaches us that there's more to this relationship than sitting around and worshiping our Savior. I understand that my salvation isn't based on my works, but I know that it's by my works that the world may also know him the way that I do. So I've never thought about questioning my motives for my servanthood.

But somehow certain questions like the one that I was about to encounter seemed to elude me.

I don't even remember what specifically triggered me to ask myself this specific question. What I do remember is that my wife and I were taking a class on spiritual healing. It was a fascinating class that helped people get to the root of issues they have in their lives that affect how and why we behave the way we do today. And as I learned that our relationship with God the Father is influenced by our relationship with our earthly father, I found myself asking, *Why do I work so hard when it comes to my relationship with God?*

THE SOLICITOUS SON

Growing up, I never had much of a strong father-figure presence in my life. My mother and birth father separated and divorced when I was just a baby. My mother remarried when I was still a young boy, and we moved over twelve hundred miles away from my birth home (and father). Mom and Dad #2 then separated and divorced when I was ten. After that, I was the man of the house for about five years, until Mom married again to a man whom I would never be able to please.

As an adult, I've worked to establish a deeper relationship with my birth father. He's a good man, and we get along really well. However, the distance (geographic and emotional) has proven difficult to overcome. He has only ever met one of my two children. And communications back and forth are spotty at best. I know that it's a two-way street. But I've always longed for a father who would show interest in my life.

Maybe that's why I strive so hard with God. Maybe I'm crying out to him and screaming, "HEY! LOOK AT ME, DADDY!" Maybe I'm doing it more than just with God. Maybe if I do something awesome enough, then both heavenly and earthly Daddy will notice me.

That's when it hit me. It sucks feeling like you're invisible.

FINDING PEACE AND LOOKING FORWARD

As I sit here at my computer, my eighteen-month-old daughter dances outside my office door shouting, "Babe! (what she calls me since learning that this is what my wife calls me) Look!" She wants me to watch her dance. Off in the distance I see my nine-year-old son jumping around, trying to steal the show. He's not saying "Look at me" with his words, but his actions speak louder than any word ever could.

One thing that my children covet from me is my attention. I can relate.

As I watch them dance, I think about how I want them to know that they never have to perform for my attention—or my acceptance. I want them to know that I'll always be there for them and that I'll always be their biggest cheerleader. I want them to know that my love for them is ever present no matter what they may do (or not do). I want them to know that I'm always looking their way.

Maybe that's how Daddy feels about me too.

THE CUP

Jennifer Dukes Lee

HER TEARS FALL EVERY TIME she holds that ruby-filled cup at the front of our sanctuary in this simple country church by the cornfield.

I don't know if anyone else notices her tears. But I do. I watch for them. That woman in the front—standing under the wooden cross on the wall—is my dearest friend. She is my covenant sister, my very own Jonathan. This morning, I'm sitting in the far back of the sanctuary, by the church's soundboard, under our white steeple. I probably ought to be praying or reciting a creed or adjusting the volume, but I can't help it: I am watching her, how she cradles one golden chalice in her hands before the Lord's Supper begins.

She knows the cost of the cup. And she says the cup always makes her cry—a quiet, grateful cry right in front of God and everybody.

I think this explains a lot about Michelle, and it explains a lot about the kind of friend that I try to be. It definitely explains who Michelle has been to me: an ambassador of her Savior. It's why she reached out to me the way she did eleven years ago in that moment she found me, shoulders slumped and spirits sagged right here in this church. All these years later, she continues to pour so much of herself into me, even on my ugliest days. It's because of the cup.

I hope that I've done the same for her.

I adjust the volume on the pastor's microphone and scroll through my iTunes library, searching for the right song to play during this morning's celebration of the Lord's Supper. Quiet strains of "I Stand Amazed" rise above the farmers with their slicked-back hair and over the top of the mothers feeding dry Cheerios from Ziploc baggies to their toddlers. The song slides up and around us all like a silk ribbon, tying together a room full of grace-hungry sinners-made-saints. This is the body of Christ, connected.

The pastor summons this community of believers forward, toward bread and wine. I rise.

Words are etched into the wooden altar up front: "Do This in Remembrance of Me." So I do. I remember.

It was under this roof, eleven years ago, when Michelle saw me sitting in one of the folding chairs by the church kitchen. I remember how she really *saw* me. She saw through my cautious smile, the carefully applied blush on my cheekbones. She saw my posture and the dark circles, earned after another sleepless night with a colicky baby. Michelle walked straight into my loneliness and insecurity and bone-tiredness. I was the new woman in town, in my husband's hometown, on his family farm, in this corner of the world where everybody already belonged. I wasn't yet sure where I fit—or even *if* I fit. And what was the body of Christ anyway?

For most of our married life up to that point, my husband and I had lived in metropolitan areas. My heart felt like it matched the pulse of the faster-paced city life. Maybe my heart felt like it could hide better in the city too. I was a busy news reporter, with little time to share my innermost heart with anyone. As a journalist, I felt more comfortable asking the questions than answering them. My reporter's notebook was like a shield, deflecting anyone if the tables were turned.

I liked it that way. I liked keeping my doubt-filled heart isolated from the scrutiny of others. If I let anyone get too close, they might see my deep anxiety over my inevitable death, my troubling uncertainty about the existence of God, and a hundred other lesser insecurities about life and faith and being mortal on planet Earth.

But the city lights had long dimmed from my life. And here I was in rural Iowa, in a tiny country church, slumped in a folding chair, with faces I didn't recognize and a faith that was still trying to wrap itself around my heart. Michelle cut straight across the room to find me. I remember how I sucked in my stomach, smoothed down my skirt and sat up straighter.

She was gorgeous, thin and tall. She wore cute jeans, a perfectly coiffed hairstyle and a slash of bright pink lipstick. I was frumpy and pudgy with a newborn in my arms.

"We should get together sometime," she said, holding out her arms so she could cradle my baby for a while.

"Yeah, that would be nice. We should get together." I nodded politely, handing over my baby girl for a moment but not believing that she'd ever really call.

Two days later, the phone rang. It was Michelle. She and her husband asked our family of four over for dinner. *That very night.*

We went, and it felt good. And they asked us for dinner again. And again. And before long, she and her husband were probing deeper, asking us about our lives, our faith and our hearts. Soon we were doing the same of them.

It felt like something holy was growing, a bit like that covenantal friendship I'd read about between David and Jonathan. It was the sort of relationship I had longed for. I was surprised by how safe it felt to get gut-level honest with someone. I risked telling her about my doubts, and she didn't judge—or back away. She listened and kept moving closer.

I knew this was a rare gift.

I had read a lot over the years about how important it was for the body of Christ to "get real with one another," to "show your true selves" and to "be authentic." At the time, those sounded like convenient buzzwords to make the church appear more welcoming than it actually was. Honestly, I didn't believe that this sort of vulnerability existed in the church. I had seen too many people get burned that way, by exposing their hurts and failures. Here's why: the church seemed okay with broken people at first, embracing them in that highly emotional moment when initial confessions were made and tears were shed. But if the broken ones didn't "fix" quickly, a few of the initial empathizers in the group gradually grew uncomfortable, and then a few more grew weary. And soon, people disappeared altogether, leaving the hurting ones doubly hurt. That's how it looked from my seat anyway, though I confess I had a jaded view back then.

Regardless, I do know this now: getting soul bare only works if someone stays by your side for the long haul, not only for the short spurt in the confession booth. Otherwise, it's just another episode of Jerry Springer, when the studio audience disappears after the hour is up.

Getting soul bare also means that we treat people like friends, not charity cases or mission "projects." This is what Christ taught with his life and with his words, even on the very night he was betrayed—the night he lifted the cup with friends.

Greater love has no one than this, that he lay down his life for his friends. You are my friends if you do what I command. (Jn 15:13-14 NIV 1984)

Here in my country church, during this celebration of the Lord's Supper, the song "I Stand Amazed" still echoes through the sanctuary. I am among the redeemed, a friend of God, shuffling toward loaf and cup.

I can see how Michelle cradles the golden cup in her hands like it's the most valuable thing she's ever held in her life—not because of what's on the outside, but what's on the inside.

One by one, the farmers and the widows and the young mothers rip bread from the loaf and then dip it into the cup she holds.

She looks everyone in the eye—every single one of us. And she's saying our names. She's making it personal:

"The blood of Christ shed for YOU, Rosie."

"The blood of Christ shed for YOU, Helmer."

For Wanda. For Bill. For Trish. For Steve. For everyone.

That one song hums in the background: "He took my sin and my sorrow, and made them his very own. He bore the burden to Calvary, and suffered and died alone."

And here I am, standing among the body of Christ, which is God's way of making sure we are never alone in this world. We were made for community, for connectedness. And the body of Christ is also this: it is Christ's *body*, given for me.

I grab a chunk of bread—a generous chunk because I want to remember what this cost. Then I sidestep to the left, toward Michelle. She holds out the cup, and there are years of history here between us, years of what it means to be a friend and to follow Christ alongside each other—how we were meant to weep together and to laugh and to dig into the Word in a very personal way and to act like complete dorks in a Target aisle. And the thing is, it's not always going to be perfect, but this is the beauty of growing together in community, rubbing up against each other and offering enough grace to let someone make mistakes, then loving one another when we repeat some of those mistakes again.

I hold in my fingers the bread, the body of Christ.

Michelle is holding the cup out to me, waiting. Tears start for both of us.

"Every time, Jennifer . . ." she says, "I can't help it."

"I know; I know" is all I can manage.

I linger long in that one spot, put my right hand on her left hand, and then, at last, I dip into the cup. She says the words to me: "The blood of Christ given for YOU, Jennifer."

And I taste grace once again. It tastes like the slow burn of wine and the salt from my very own tears, let loose by a cup in the hands of a friend.

LOST AND FOUND

Cara Sexton

L IKE MOST CHRISTIANS, I HAVE MY OWN before-and-after-redemption testimony. I was fourteen when I met Jesus at a Christian summer camp. It was the year I'd started secretly cutting myself with a rusty X-Acto knife after sneaking shots of vodka from the jug in our cupboard. It was the year I'd kept myself distracted enough to numb the boredom of my after-school janitor job by carefully plotting the details of my suicide while I vacuumed junior high classrooms. It was a secret nobody could have suspected—I have always been particularly skilled at putting on a happy face—and while I desperately needed saving, nobody could have helped me. Nobody could have ever known the torment going on within me, the battles waged behind my smile.

And then, as a good testimony goes, I found the church—or rather, the church found me—and through it, the hope of God, who found me on my knees on a summer night saying an impassioned yes.

I was blind but now I see.

It stopped for a while, the razor blades and vodka shots. I began memorizing Scripture and serving on a church leadership team instead of dreaming up new ways to die.

And there he was, *Amazing Grace, who saved a wretch like me.* In popular Christian subculture, this is where the testimony ends. This is where the clapping begins and the band plays softly and we all give praise because of how Jesus saves. But this, like many things with good intentions, also carries with it a lie of omission that eventually marginalizes so many of us for whom salvation does not look like a one-and-done life makeover. Some of us still battle on our knees every day. Some of us have wounds that survived baptismal waters.

I'm thirty-six now and I have spent a lifetime in Christian churches, in ministry, in the ups and downs of life that didn't stop once I began wearing a rhinestone cross around my neck. I know Jesus. I have walked the "Roman road" up and down so many times I can do it with my eyes closed. I have prayed the prayers of a lost soul. I have been baptized (twice, in case the first time didn't take). I've turned to books, experts, pastors and every Christian resource I could find, and they've all seemed to suggest that if only I could believe more, try harder, schedule enough early morning "quiet times," pray the right prayer or serve with more fervor that my faith will be restored. I've found nothing on the shelves to tell a desperate soul what to do when they once were lost and then they became lost again. Nothing I've picked up seems to go beyond the all-cleaned-up-for-church façade that faith is something you put on your calendar, something you do, something that, if only you search hard enough, you can locate.

But I have never found redemption to work with the simple math that has always seemed suggestive of the Christian life, the formula written on my notebook during one high school retreat by a well-meaning youth pastor: You + Jesus = Enough.

Have you ever felt like the road to redemption wasn't that easy? Have you ever felt like you can know Jesus and still be a heap of hot mess? Like a prayer of salvation wasn't enough to fix what was broken within you once and for all?

I once was lost . . .

I still am.

Was blind . . .

On my good days I can make out the shape of a holy God somewhere in the distance. On the bad ones, it's still just a lot of haze. This is maybe the worst place from which to write about the redemption of God.

But then again, maybe not.

I struggle with severe chronic illness—a combination of painful autoimmune conditions that often makes climbing a flight of stairs or using a can opener feel like my bones have turned into razor blades. There are days, increasingly more lately, when I can barely get out of bed simply because my inflamed spine cannot handle the stress of sitting in a chair, my knees cannot manage the staircase to the kitchen. I am on a chemotherapy drug that keeps me feeling weak and nauseated, and a cocktail of pills morning, noon and night to try and keep the damage at bay. So far, they don't seem to be working. Coming to terms with the recent loss of my functionality has been nothing short of heart-breaking. It has triggered depression and anxiety to go along with the physical struggle.

Although I have often seen the hand of God directly in the midst of my pain, the combination of crushing challenges has wreaked havoc on my faith. My song of praise has often sounded more like a battle cry. Not long ago, I found myself in bed in a heap of tears, my stomach gnawing, my spirit empty. My Bible sat on a high shelf above me and I stared at it, trying to remember the last time I'd even taken it down. Had it gathered dust? Maybe so. But brimming with pain, anger and confusion, I didn't have the strength to open it. I couldn't, in the state I was in, drag myself to the foot of the cross. I laid there trying to find words with which to pray, but nothing came. I had only a broken spirit, a tired body, a mouth that could form nothing short of defeated breaths, chapped lips salty with my own hot tears. My prayer that night sounded only like, "Help." It was all I had the strength for. It was all I knew how to say.

What I want to tell you is that the heavens split open, that a hand reached down and rescued me. I want to say that I prayed a prayer and all my hurt disappeared, that I woke up in the morning healed of all my pain. I want to say that my whole hot mess of a self was swirled up in a cloud of starry magic and bibbidi-bobbidi-boo, I was better. I want to say I was *found*.

But that is not what happened. Jesus did not throw my bedroom door wide and cast out all my pain, no matter how my silent suffering had urged him to, because this is usually not the way it works. The truth is rarely easy. It is not cleaned up for church. It is raw and regular and real. And it is, sometimes, the only way we can show up. Soul bare. Broken and bloody and without an ounce of hope.

What I needed that night, while I lay in the fetal position on my bed, was a miracle. I needed the sky to rip open and everything in my world to change because I just could not take one more second of the pain I was in. I needed a trumpet. I needed an angel. I needed my own fingers in the scarred palm of Christ or I might not have been able to continue believing at all. I needed something so tangible that I could not resist the power of its healing.

What I got was Batman.

My bedroom door cracked open. A blonde boy in footie pajamas, my youngest son, Caleb, shuffled in and looked at me with all the love you could ever gather into two green eyes. He didn't seem to notice the way my face was puffed from crying, my lifeless body barely hanging on. He seemed to see something beautiful.

"I love you around my heart and back," he said with a smile.

"Oh yeah? Well *I* love *you* around the whole universe and back. *Twice.*"

"Well. *I* love *you* around the whole entire *time* and back. Ten times!" he said, holding up all his fingers, spread wide to demonstrate the enormity of his one-uppance.

"I guess you win," I said with pretend defeat.

He giggled a perfect first-grade giggle and threw his arms around me. His impossibly long eyelashes tickled my face. Freckled across the bridge of his nose was a constellation of hope where every beautiful thing in the world was painted.

And then, he sang.

At first, I hadn't noticed the song—I was too focused on his freckles, on the way he looked at me. I was too washed away by the wave of truth that had spread over me until I heard the words to a song I wasn't even aware he knew.

There stood my baby Batman, singing, soft and true, "Amazing grace, how sweet the sound . . ."

I once was lost but now am found, was blind but now I see—that the tiniest, most innocent thing in the world can overcome the greatest of impossibilities. I am reminded that being saved by grace is a matter of paying attention to the poetic beauty of the way redemption works. *How sweet the sound* indeed.

By the time his song was done, the kisses were delivered, and the tucking in performed, I believed in something again. I believed in freckles. I believed in Batman. I believed in "Help."

Jesus did not throw a door wide for a way out. He did not give me an answer or a cure. He did not take my pain away. He did not wave a magic wand and dissipate the hard from this life.

He gave me round green eyes looking back at me with love. He gave me just enough breath in my lungs to get through the night. And in the morning, there was the sun. There were clouds. There were leaves, diaphanous and yellow and floating off trees. There was enough beauty to get through the minute and then to get through the hour and then to get through the day.

I believe that we have done damage in a Christian culture of recruiting new believers with the illusion that once they pray for salvation, everything changes. It does, of course, but it also doesn't. Our lives still fall apart. Loved ones die. Spouses leave. Flat tires and bad timing and unfortunate lab results still occur and they are not marks of failure in our spiritual lives, though we often process them as such.

I've heard it said, "Jesus doesn't promise us it will be easy, He promises us it'll be worth it." I disagree. The very idea of worth suggests that this is a thing that can be earned by our goodness, our holy service, our money, our faithful acts, our striving after God. But it has taken me twenty-two years of chasing after Jesus to learn that coming to faith is not like climbing a ladder; it is, instead, like falling from one. We arrive at the throne of God not by our own acts of will, not by our wise decisions, not by our goodness. We arrive at redemptive grace when we have finally admitted we have nowhere else to go. We arrive at the throne of grace when our knees are bleeding and we finally say "Help."

This is what it means to be soul bare. This is what it means to seek God with all our heart and mind and soul. It does not mean, as anyone who has ever lingered in Christian subculture may suspect, that we have reached a pinnacle of faith—that we have simply believed hard enough.

It is to be lost and found, over and over and over again. It is to recognize the upside-down nature of the things of this world. It is to know that even when we are lost, we have a finding place. It is to know the word *help*.

Even when we have no words, even when we have only blindness and cannot take ourselves to the Word made flesh, he comes anyhow, somehow. He comes, and a splash of freckles holds all the hope of heaven on earth. He comes, and against all odds, *we see*.

ACKNOWLEDGMENTS

When you are a Bear of Very Little Brain, and you
Think of Things, you find sometimes that a Thing which
seemed very Thingish inside you is quite different when it
gets out into the open and has other people looking at it.

A. A. MILNE, *WINNIE-THE-POOH*

IT IS SO SURREAL TO ALL OF US that this Thingish *Think* is now a Thingish *Thing* you are holding in your actual hands: a book full of stories that were tucked in the corners of dark places and are now shedding light in the world several years after this idea was first born. Things did not always go as planned. Redemption is messy business. So is birth. So is faith. So is storytelling. None of us could have gathered the strength to put our shaky souls onto the page without the incredible support of our friends, family, communities and loved ones. Thank you for all you have given.

To each of the incredible, gifted contributors: from the very first heartbeat of this project, it has been for you and from the very heart of God. This book was an act of supernatural love and nothing less. May these collective words always remind you of Whose you are. Thank you for your enduring patience, your selfless gift, and especially for the privilege of being a midwife to these beautiful and bloody, screaming and glorious stories that came from your very own flesh, your soul laid bare. This book belongs to you.

To Chip MacGregor and MacGregor Literary for seeing straight to the heart of this work from the very beginning and making this big dream come true. To Helen Lee, Ellen Hsu, Lorraine Caulton, Nathan Baker-Lutz and everyone at InterVarsity Press for catching our vision and making it your own. To Help One Now for allowing us to partner with the amazing work you are doing in this world.

To my husband, Ryan: your endless support, steadfast patience, and selfless nature are, along with our children, the greatest gifts I have in this life. Caedon, Kennedy, Caleb and Jacob: Thank you for giving up your mama more than was fair so I could help nurture this thing into the world. I love you all the way and back. Amy Lou, you are my favorite and my best. Mom and Ben, Paige, Kilani and Mark, Dani Sue, Tom, Craig Wright, Randi, Ginny, Sunny, Mindy, Wayne, Clint, Jennifer, Brandy, Janel, Adrian, Bobby, Elizabeth, Tina, Jessica, Tammy, Teresa, Dad, my *entire* Goddard family and the countless other cheerleaders, prayer warriors and angels who whispered in my ear when the going got tough, "keep going; this matters." If not for you, this would still be a what-if. Thank you, thank you, thank you.

And lastly, but most importantly, to you, reader: Thank you for reading our stories. I hope they have changed you or encouraged you. May your heart be flooded, always, by the great love of a Father who is always beyond your comprehension but never beyond your reach. May your eyes and hearts and souls be bare before God and one another, and may we all walk together, hand in hand, into this great love.

Join the Conversation: #SoulBare.

NOTES

DARK CLOUDS AND ABUNDANT GRACE

24   *Hymn writer William Cowper*: "God Moves in a Mysterious Way," www.cyberhymnal.org/htm/g/m/gmovesmw.htm.

COLD, DARK GROUND

27   *In C. S. Lewis's*: *The Great Divorce* (New York: Macmillan, 1946).

JOY TO THE WORLD! REALLY? WHERE?

82   *Good-by, good-by*: Thornton Wilder, *Our Town* (New York: Avon, 1975).

WRESTLING WITH GOD IN THE ART HOUSE THEATER

103   *Paschal Hymn*: V. Rev. Father Joseph Rahal, ed., *The Services of Great and Holy Week and Pascha* (Englewood, NJ: Antakya Press, 2006).

BREATHING ROOM

121   *Room*: Emma Donoghue, *Room: A Novel* (New York: Little, Brown, 2010).

THE CHOREOGRAPHY OF GOD

159   *Writing is a process*: Henri Nouwen, "Theology as Doxology: Reflections on Theological Education," in *Caring for the Commonweal: Education for Religious and Public Life*, ed. Parker J. Palmer, Barbara G. Wheeler and James W. Fowler (Macon, GA: Mercer University Press, 1990).

160   *put [my] ear down*: Anne Sexton. Original source unknown.

YOU'RE NOT ALONE

166   *Love anything and*: C. S. Lewis, *The Four Loves* (New York: Harcourt, Brace, 1960).

GRAVITY

174   *allowing that which is*: Ruth Haley Barton, *Invitation to Solitude and Silence* (Downers Grove, IL: InterVarsity Press, 2004), 33.

MEET THE AUTHORS

Cara Sexton (introduction, "Lost and Found") describes herself as "part monk, part punk." She lives with her husband and four children in beautiful southern Oregon where she cultivates a passion for creativity and inspiration as she daily gathers the manna of ordinary magic from even the unlikeliest of places. Cara writes creative nonfiction, poetry and fiction, and her work has appeared in the books *Finding Church* and *What a Woman is Worth* as well as in many magazines and online publications. She has worked as nonfiction editor for *Duende* literary magazine and is currently writing a spiritual memoir while completing her BFA degree in creative writing at Goddard College. When she isn't writing, she is probably decorating, daydreaming, kissing freckles, scouring flea markets for vintage trinkets or preparing for her next big adventure. You can (try to) keep up with her at carasexton.com.

Linda Basmeson ("The Yearbook") is a single mother of two teens living in south Florida. By day she is a counselor and schoolteacher. By night she is a dreamer, blogger and unofficial, semiprofessional coffee shop critic. Linda understands the challenges of being a single mom with a type-A personality. Her heart is to see women come to know Christ personally and to genuinely open their hearts to his limitless love. Find her at radiantjoy.org.

Joy Bennett ("Metamorphosis") has over seventeen years of experience as a professional writer. She consults with businesses and nonprofits around the world (tech, manufacturing, transportation, finance, health care, humanitarian), seeking to tell their stories and woo supporters in authentic and compelling ways. She has traveled internationally and presented at conferences, in boardrooms and via webinar on everything from branding to bedside manner. She is married with four children, three living. You can connect with her online at joywbennett. com and @writingjoy on Twitter.

Sarah Bessey ("Letters of Intention") is a writer and blogger. She is a happy-clappy Jesus lover, a joyful subversive and a social justice wanna-be trying to do a bit of good. She lives in Abbotsford, British Columbia, with her husband, Brian, and their four tinies: Anne, Joseph, Evelynn and Margaret Love. She is the author of *Jesus Feminist* and *Out of Sorts*. You can find her online at sarahbessey.com.

Kris Camealy ("Captivity"): As a sequin-wearing, homeschooling mother of four, Kris is passionate about Jesus, people and words. Her heart beats to share the hard but glorious truth about life in Christ. She's been known to take gratuitous pictures of her culinary creations, causing mouths to water all across Instagram. Once upon a time, she ran ten miles for Compassion International, a ministry for which she serves as an advocate. Kris is the author of *Holey, Wholly, Holy: A Lenten Journey* *of Refinement* and the follow up *Companion Workbook.* She spends her free time managing gracetable.org and occasionally writing at kriscamealy.com.

Jennifer J. Camp ("Cold, Dark Ground") is the author of *Loop: What Women Need to Know* and cofounder of Gather Ministries with her husband, Justin. She lives in the San Francisco Bay Area with her husband, three kids and very insecure dog. Her favorite thing to do? Listen to God's voice in her life and encourage women to wake to the full life he invites us to have. Follow her writing and get updates on her upcoming book at gatherministries.com and jenniferjcamp.com.

Deana Chadwell ("Joy to the World! Really? Where?") is an award-winning poet and author of a poetry chapbook titled *Counterpane.* She blogs at *A Single Window* (asinglewindow.com) and also publishes at Stubborn Things (stubbornthings.org) and American Thinker (americanthinker.com). She currently teaches writing at Pacific Bible College. Deana lives in southern Oregon with her husband. In her spare time she enjoys needlework and jewelry design, cooking and entertaining.

Emily P. Freeman ("Gravity") is the author of several books, including two *Wall Street Journal*–bestsellers, *Grace for the Good Girl* and *Simply Tuesday.* For over ten years she's been quietly writing online at emilypfreeman.com, where she is all about creating space for the soul to breathe. Emily and her husband, John, live in North Carolina with their three children. Connect with her on Twitter and Instagram: @emilypfreeman.

Holley Gerth ("You're Not Alone") is the bestselling author of *You're Already Amazing* and several other books. She's also a life coach, speaker and cofounder of www.incourage.me. You can find her online at holleygerth.com. Holley lives in the South where she shares her heart and home with her husband, Mark.

Christina Gibson ("Pain and Holy Ground") is a teacher, preacher and writer. She grew up in Colorado and studied at Baylor and Truett Theological Seminary. Christina speaks and preaches at churches across the country and is currently finishing up an in-depth study of Exodus. She loves laughing with her pastor husband and three small children and enjoys her work as a fitness instructor. When she's not blogging (christinamaygibson.com), she spends her free time trying to take a nap.

Holly Grantham ("The Choreography of God"): After years in Atlanta, where she attended college, married the love of her life and lived in an intentional community, she found her way back to her home state of Missouri. She now lives in an antebellum stone house and homeschools her three boys. She is a writer and editor for *SheLoves* magazine and blogs at *A Lifetime of Days* (walkingintheslowlane.blogspot.com). Follow Holly on Twitter: @HollyAGrantham.

Seth Haines ("Nuance") is a working stiff who makes his home in the Ozark Mountains. He and his wife, Amber Haines, have four boys and a dog named Lucy. Seth enjoys music, food, fly fishing and fine sentences. He is the author of *Coming Clean*, a story of pain, faith and the abiding love of God. You can find him at sethhaines.com, or on Twitter, @sethhaines.

Angie Hong ("The Root") is a mom, wife and worship leader currently residing in Chicago. Angie is the main facilitator of Menders, a worship band exploring the intersection of worship and reconciliation. She blogs about identity, worship and reconciliation at angiekayhong.com. Angie also leads worship at national conferences and speaks about worship and reconciliation.

Dan King ("Look at Me, Daddy!") serves as Patheos Faith and Work Channel editor for The High Calling, blogger at bibledude.net and President of Fistbump Media, LLC. He's author of *The Unlikely Missionary* and *Activist Faith*. He lives in Sarasota, Florida, with his wife, Krista, and their two children. You can connect with him on Twitter: @bibledude.

Sheila Seiler Lagrand ("Striptease") and her husband, Rich, live with their three dogs in beautiful Trabuco Canyon, California. Sheila is an anthropologist by training, and her current projects include a book about grandparenting and another about recess—for adults. Her novel *Remembering for Ruth* was released in 2014. She enjoys writing, doodling and indulging her grand-littles. Find her at sheilalagrand.com.

Jennifer Dukes Lee ("The Cup") is the author of *Love Idol*. She's a writer for Dayspring's (in)courage and a community editor for The High Calling. She's a grace dweller and storyteller, writing regularly at her blog, jenniferdukeslee.com.

Sarah Markley ("Without People Like You") lives in Orange County, California, with her husband and two daughters and is a work-at-home mother, managing two part-time nonprofit jobs and a household. She leads a vibrant writing life and has often said that writing is God's thoroughfare to her heart. She plays Christmas music in August, wishes she could open a bakery and loves to share her table with friends, wine and good food as much as possible.

Tanya Marlow ("Breathing Room"), writer and author of *Coming Back to God When You Feel Empty*, has ten years' experience as a

Christian minister, pastoral counselor and lecturer in biblical theology. She loves opera singing, dark chocolate and laughing at her own jokes. She lives in a vicarage in Devon, England, with her husband and energetic son and writes at tanyamarlow.com.

Shannan Martin ("More for You Than This") is a writer who found her voice in the country and her story in the city. She and her jail chaplain husband have four funny children who came to them across oceans and rivers. Having sold their American Dream, they now live entrenched in community on the wrong side of the tracks. Shannan was rescued from the life she thought she wanted and is surprised every day by God's goodness. She blogs at flowerpatchfarmgirl.com.

Shelly Miller ("Redemption Looks Beautiful on You") is smitten with the power of story to make people think differently and is the founder of the Sabbath Society. Described as a poet with an acute taste for authentic honesty, she is a friend to the layman who searches for hope. Her writing is featured in a number of magazines, books and websites and weekly on her blog, *Redemption's Beauty*.

Trillia J. Newbell ("Dark Clouds and Abundant Grace") is the author of *Fear and Faith: Finding the Peace Your Heart Craves* and *United: Captured by God's Vision for Diversity*. Her writings on issues of faith, family and diversity have been published in the *Knoxville News-Sentinel, Desiring God, Christianity Today, Relevant Magazine,* The Gospel Coalition and more. She is currently director of community outreach for the Ethics and Religious Liberty Commission for the Southern Baptist Convention. Along with writing, she is pursuing her MA in biblical counseling from Southern Theological Seminary. For fun, she enjoys group fitness (she used to be a fitness instructor!), cycling and listening to a variety of music. Trillia is married to her best friend, Thern, and they reside with their two children near Nashville. You can find her at trillianewbell.com and follow her on Twitter, @trillianewbell.

Tammy Perlmutter ("The Waging and the Waiting") writes about unabridged life, fragmented faith and investing in the mess at her blog *Raggle-Taggle*. She recently launched a collaborative space, The Mudroom, making room for people who need a place to be fully themselves. Tammy writes guest posts, personal essays, flash memoir and poetry, and preaches sometimes. She lives in Chicago with her husband, Mike, and daughter, Phoenix.

Amy Peterson ("Teenage Heretic") is a writer, ESL instructor and mother of two. She works with the Honors Guild at Taylor University and is interested in education, mothering, books, theology, intercultural communication, food, pop culture and any combination thereof. She blogs occasionally at amypeterson.net.

Tara Pohlkotte ("Tie to the Deep") is a writer, mother of two sweet souls and lover of simple beauty. Named one of BlogHer's 2013 Voices of the Year, she is a published poet and author. Her most recent work is a small collection of poetry and essays surrounding motherhood titled *Dreamcatcher*.

Monica Sharman ("When I Pursued Joy") is a home educator, a freelance editor and the author of *Behold the Beauty: An Invitation to Bible Reading* (forthcoming). She lives in Colorado with her husband, the inventor of Crossbeams Toy, and three sons. She delights in children's fiction, poetry and drumming. Connect with Monica on Twitter, @monicasharman and at monicasharman.wordpress.com.

Amy Smith ("Liquid Courage") is a married to her high school sweetheart, has nine kids, and yes, she knows what causes that. She paints, reads and writes in equal parts, and has an affinity for 80s music, coffee, chocolate, wine and developing annoying nicknames for her besties, but she loves Jesus most of all. Find her at alovestoryinthelilies.blogspot.com.

Karissa Knox Sorrell ("Wrestling with God in the Art House Theater") is a writer, poet and ESL educator from Nashville, Tennessee. Her poetry and creative nonfiction have been seen in *St. Katherine Review, Relief Journal, Rock & Sling* blog, *San Pedro River Review, Parable Press, Silver Birch Press* and *Cactus Heart*, among others. Her poetry chapbook, *Evening Body*, is forthcoming. When not writing, Karissa trains and mentors ESL teachers in Metro Nashville Public Schools. Karissa writes about reading, writing and faith wrestling at her blog, karissaknoxsorrell.com. You can follow her on Twitter: @KKSorrell.

Mandy Steward ("Breathing Fresh Air") is an artist, writer and teacher. She teaches art locally and online and runs a correspondence school called The Magic School. She blogs regularly at messycanvas.com. She also self-publishes a subscription-based zine for artists called the *Secret Message Society*. Steward has written a spiritual memoir called *Thrashing About with God: Finding Faith on the Other Side of Everything*. She attributes her personal freedom to the process of writing that book.

Lindsey van Niekerk ("A Broken Love Story"): Growing up as a missionary kid in Haiti defined much of Lindsey's life. After earning her degree in psychology and communications, she spent ten years serving in full-time ministry. Lindsey and her long-awaited South African McDreamy now find themselves living life on indefinite sabbatical and basking daily in the knowledge of God's radical love and grace. During this unknown season, God broke their hearts wide open through foster care and later the adoption of their now energetic, spirited, lover-of-life toddler, Maya Grace. Lindsey writes as The Little Missionary Girl All Grown Up at her personal blog, lindseyvanniekerk.blogspot.com.

Kelli Woodford ("Of Old Mirrors and New Doors") lives in the Midwest, surrounded by cornfields and love, with her husband and seven blue-eyed children. They laugh, play, fight and mend, but they don't do anything that even slightly resembles quiet. Unless it's listening to their lives, which has proved to be the biggest challenge of them all.

Serena Woods ("Towers and Canyons") is a thinker who writes for various publications, on- and offline. She's an advocate for grace and writes her argument for gospel at graceisforsinners.com.

HELPONENOW

Help One Now is a catalytic tribe committed to empowering and resourcing high-capacity local leaders who care for orphans and vulnerable children in order to transform communities and break the cycle of extreme poverty. A portion of the proceeds of *Soul Bare* will support this work.

The leaders we support are already working effectively in their respective communities. In other words, they're not waiting for us—they already have the passion and history of doing the hard work of community transformation. We work with them, walk alongside them, encourage them, equip them, pray for them and serve them in their greatest areas of need. These leaders are friends and partners in the fight against extreme poverty. They are our greatest resource, and without them sustainable change is impossible.

As a collective group of churches, businesses, communities and individuals from around the world, we are deeply committed to using our gifts, talents and resources to fight extreme poverty, care for orphans, rescue slaves and see communities transformed through our international partners. We actively sponsor kids, host garage sales to support initiatives, donate funds, participate in life-changing trips, advocate for the vulnerable and much more.

Help One Now believes that doing good can be simple and that every person has a role to play. We are deeply committed to do good, to do it well and to do it together.

LEARN MORE AT HELPONENOW.ORG.

Together We Build!

IVP *Crescendo*
COURAGE. CONFIDENCE. CALLING.

Some voices challenge us. Others support or encourage us. Voices can move us to change our minds, draw close to God, discover a new spiritual gift. The voices of others are shaping who we are.

The voices behind IVP Crescendo join together to draw us into God's story. We'll discover God's work around the globe even as we learn to love the people around the corner. We'll have opportunity to heal our places of pain. We'll discover new ways to love our families. We'll hear God's voice speaking into our lives as we discover new places of influence.

IVP Crescendo invites you to join in the rising chorus

- *to listen to the voices of others*
- *to hear the voice of God*
- *and to grow your own voice in*

COURAGE. CONFIDENCE. CALLING.

ivpress.com/crescendo
ivpress.com/crescendo-social